Come to the
Lord's Table

Come to the Lord's Table

A Sacred Assembly for the Church

Claude King

with meditations by
Andrew Murray
from *The Lord's Table*

FINAL COMMAND RESOURCES™
Murfreesboro, Tennessee

In 1897 Andrew Murray published *The Lord's Table: A Help to the Right Observance of the Holy Supper.* Meditations from *The Lord's Table* have been updated and edited by Claude King. They will be identified by indention from the left margin in smaller type and with the reference: (*LT*, p. #). A complete public domain text of *The Lord's Table* by Murray is available on the Internet at: http://www.ccel.org/m/murray/lords_table/ and can be printed out for your own use or for distribution to others. *The Lord's Table* is also available in book form (published by The Christian Literature Crusade).

The Scriptures used in Andrew Murray's meditations are revised from the public domain text of *The Lord's Table* which was originally written in Dutch and then translated into English. When referenced in this book, those Scriptures are marked AM.

The front cover painting was commissioned from ArtSorce.com.

ISBN 0-9651288-3-0

3 4 5 6 7 8 9 10 — 05

Printed in the USA

For information regarding language translations, overseas publication rights, or customized editions contact the publisher by mail at the address below or by e-mail at: info@FinalCommand.org. Please note that we do not accept unsolicited manuscripts.

Published by
Final Command Resources™
P. O. Box 332503
Murfreesboro, TN 37133-2503

Order bulk quantities at www.FinalCommand.org

CONTENTS

PREFACE

In 1989 Richard Owen Roberts of Wheaton, Illinois, introduced me and other leaders in my denomination to the biblical pattern for corporate repentance—the solemn assembly (or "sacred" assembly in the *New International Version*).[1] We began to study sacred assemblies in Scripture to see their connections to revival. Sacred assemblies were occasions for God's people collectively to worship Him, to repent of personal and corporate sin, to remember His special blessings on them, and to anticipate future blessings. The prescribed sacred assemblies (or holy convocations) for Israel included the Sabbath (Lev. 23:3) and seven other days of sacred assembly: the first (Passover) and seventh days of the Feast of Unleavened Bread (Lev. 23:4-8), the Feast of Weeks (Pentecost, Lev. 23:15-21), the Feast of Trumpets (Lev. 23:23-25), the Day of Atonement (Lev. 23:26-32), and the first and eighth days of the Feast of Tabernacles (Lev. 23:33-36).

Sacred assemblies were times for God's people to confess and repent of their sins. They were times to renew the covenant relationship with the Lord and return to Him in faithful love and obedience. They were times for worship and sacrifice, feasting and fasting. Even with these regular opportunities to renew fellowship with God, His people tended to depart from Him and from obedience to His commands. Spiritual leaders knew that the sacred assembly was a time for corporate repentance in the face of God's righteous judgments (see Joel 1–2). A number of national revivals in the Old Testament occurred in response to a sacred assembly.

The term "sacred assembly" is not used in the New Testament. However, Jesus and His disciples celebrated the Last Supper on one of God's prescribed sacred assemblies—the Feast of Passover. The first disciples were celebrating a sacred assembly when the Holy Spirit was poured out at Pentecost. The church of our day also needs regular opportunities for individuals and the church to renew their relationships with the Lord—to remember and renew the New Covenant relationship they have with Him. I believe the Lord's Supper or Communion is probably our best and most natural opportunity to celebrate a sacred assembly of God's people.

Churches in the past took the Lord's Supper very seriously. Many churches would take a day, a weekend, or even a week or more for special services to help God's people prepare themselves to partake of the Lord's Table in a worthy manner. These days were sometimes called "pre-Communion" days. Some groups would even "fence" the Lord's Table to prevent the event from being defiled by unworthy participants. Only those who adequately had prepared themselves were permitted to partake.

I was explaining this to a missionary from West Africa when he exclaimed, "That's what happened to me in Africa!" He went on to explain that he went to pastor a church during his first term as a missionary. One Sunday he realized the congregation had not celebrated the Lord's Supper since his arrival. He announced in the morning service that they would celebrate the Supper that evening.

An elder on the front row began to weep and said, "Pastor, you must not ask us to do this. We always spend at least a day preparing ourselves for the Lord's Supper. We haven't had time to prepare. It would be offensive to God for us to come unprepared. Please don't ask us to do this." The missionary realized that they treated the Lord's Supper with much greater respect than the ways to which he was accustomed. We need to return to celebrating the Lord's Supper in a worthy manner.

The Lord's Table is a wonderful opportunity for the church to celebrate a sacred assembly and renew their fellowship and the New Covenant with their Lord. I have designed *Come to the Lord's Table* to provide your church with a tool to help your entire congregation prepare for a special celebration of Communion (or the Lord's Supper or the Eucharist) as a sacred assembly of your church. I have provided suggestions for use of *Come to the Lord's Table* in the Pastor's Guide in the Appendix.

My prayer is that the Lord will use this simple tool to renew churches as we give special attention to remembering the Lord's death until He comes again. Take time each day using this guide to help you prepare your mind, heart, and life for your meeting at the Lord's Table. Even if you will not be able to attend the service, join your church in preparing to be a people who are pleasing to the Lord.

Claude V. King

---

[1]A pamphlet entitled "The Solemn Assembly" by Richard Owen Roberts is available from International Awakening Ministries, P. O. Box 232, Wheaton, IL 60189 (www.intl-awaken.com). Two books by Roberts (also available from IAM) that may be of special help and interest to pastors are: *Revival!* and *Sanctify the Congregation: A Call to the Solemn Assembly and to Corporate Repentance.* The latter volume includes the text of "The Solemn Assembly" pamphlet.

Week 1

❧

IN REMEMBRANCE
OF ME

*"This is my body given for you;
do this in remembrance of me."*

OVERVIEW OF WEEK 1

Day 1: Introduction to the Lord's Table
Day 2: The Last Supper
Day 3: The Wedding Supper of the Lamb
Day 4: The Divine Invitation
Day 5: From Supper to the Cross
Day 6: Broken Body and Shed Blood
Day 7: The Wounded Savior

This week you will begin your study of *Come to the Lord's Table* by focusing attention on Jesus and what He has done for you on the cross. Allow this to be a time to remember Him and to remember what He has done for you. Use this week to rekindle your first love for Jesus Christ.

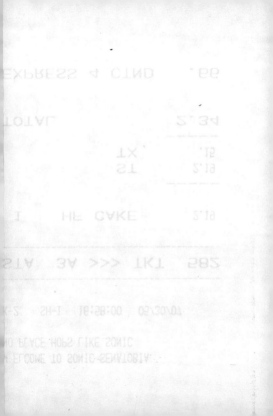

WELCOME TO SONIC SENATOBIA
NO PLACE HOPS LIKE SONIC

K-2   SH-1   16:58:00   05/30/07

STA   3A >>> TKT   582

1   HF CAKE   2.19

                ST   2.19
                TX   .15

TOTAL   2.34

EXPRESS 4 CTND   .66

Day 1

Introduction to the Lord's Table

"God so loved the world that he gave his one and only Son, that whoever believes in him shall not perish but have eternal life" (John 3:16). What good news that is for you and me! God loved us so much that He gave the life of His Son Jesus Christ so that we could know life at its best, for all eternity. Of all people on earth, we are most blessed. I don't know about you, but I'm overwhelmed to think that the Creator of the universe has such an interest in me.

But life's activities and concerns can cause us to grow casual and indifferent toward our blessed relationship with Jesus Christ. God knew that our human nature would tend to draw us away from our first love for Jesus Christ. It happens so gradually that we fail to realize what's happening until our love has grown cold. Fortunately, God loves us too much to let us drift that far away from Him without attempting to draw us back. That's why God gave us instructions for experiences that can help us remember His blessings. He guides us to renew our close fellowship with Him.

➡ **How would you rate the "warmth" of your love relationship with Jesus Christ today? Check one.**
- ❏ a. Hot. I am deeply in love with my Savior.
- ❏ b. Warm. I know a closeness to Jesus, but I've been closer.
- ❏ c. Lukewarm. I go through the motions of faithfulness, but I can't say that I have much passion for Jesus.
- ❏ d. Cold. I am pretty distant and indifferent to love for Christ.

Wherever you find yourself in your love relationship with Jesus Christ, God is reaching out to you. He is inviting you to a deeper experience of that love relationship for which Jesus Christ gave His life. Most of us would have to confess that we need to return to a deeper love for Christ.

Of all the ways we can be restored to fellowship with Christ, no experience holds more meaning or emotion for that purpose than the celebration of the Lord's Supper. Different groups call it by different names: like Communion or the Holy Eucharist. God isn't so concerned by what we call the celebration as He is that we use the experience to renew our New Covenant relationship with Jesus Christ our Savior. Probably the reason you are studying this book is because your church family has chosen to use this guide to help you prepare for an observance of the Lord's Table. Welcome!

➡ **What name does your church use for celebrating the Holy Supper that Jesus instituted on the night before the cross?**
  ❏ a. The Lord's Supper
  ❏ b. Communion
  ❏ c. Eucharist
  ❏ d. Other: _____

Different churches and Christian traditions use different names for this holy meal. I'll use the "Lord's Table" to refer to the Lord's Supper, Communion, Eucharist, or other title your church may use to describe the holy supper you celebrate.

➡ **Turn to page 112 and write down the date for your church's special celebration of the Lord's Table. (For a four-week study see p. 111.) If you also have plans for a pre-Communion service and/or a "love feast," write those dates on the lines provided. Write these dates on your personal or work calendar as well. Check here when you have recorded the dates. ❏**

➡ **Which calendar will you use? Check one.**
  ❏ a. Calendar 1 for a Sunday observance of the Supper.
  ❏ b. Calendar 2 for a Thursday observance of the Supper.
  ❏ c. Other: for an observance on (weekday) _____

➡ **You may want to write in the numbers of the days of the month on the calendar you have chosen to use. This way you can keep track of the daily lessons you will study leading up to the Lord's Table. Write them in now.**

This devotional guide has been prepared to help you and your church get ready to partake of the Lord's Table in a worthy manner. Please participate in the preparations. Make every effort to join together with your church family for this very special occasion. I recommend that you cancel or change any conflicts that would prevent your participation. For the Old Testament sacred assemblies, participants were commanded to "do no regular work" (Lev. 23:7, 8, 21, 25, 31, 35, and 36). I would recommend that you arrange to take the day off from your regular work on the day scheduled for the Lord's

Table. Give the entire day to the Lord as a sacrifice and thank offering. Another characteristic of the sacred assemblies in the Bible was that all the people who could understand were expected to attend. Plan now to join your church in this special sacred assembly.

Getting Ready to Come to the Lord's Table

Many people have a deep concern over the casual way modern Christians participate in the Lord's Table. Paul's warning to the Corinthians *should* cause us to be concerned:

> Whoever eats the bread or drinks the cup of the Lord in an unworthy manner will be guilty of sinning against the body and blood of the Lord. A man ought to examine himself before he eats of the bread and drinks of the cup. For anyone who eats and drinks without recognizing the body of the Lord eats and drinks judgment on himself. That is why many among you are weak and sick, and a number of you have fallen asleep (1 Cor. 11:27-30).

Have you ever gone to the Lord's Table to partake of the bread and juice (or wine) and left the service unmoved and unchanged? I have. However, when I partake of the Supper in a casual way, I unintentionally say, "Lord, Your death on the cross wasn't that important." How grieved God must be when I care so little for the great sacrifice He paid for my salvation.

In 1897 famed author and pastor Andrew Murray of South Africa wrote a book for his congregation to help them observe the "Holy Supper" in a worthy manner. Members spent a week prior to the Supper in personal preparation using Murray's book *The Lord's Table* as their devotional guide. The book provided prayers and meditations for the day of the celebration. Then members spent the week following the celebration reflecting on the changes that should take place in their lives because of the sacrifice Christ had made for them.

When I first read *The Lord's Table*, I realized we needed a similar work for the churches of our day. In his preface Murray said,

> I am convinced that one chief cause why some do not grow more in grace is that they do not take time to converse with the Lord in secret. Spiritual, divine truth does not become my possession all at once. Although I understand what I read, although I consent heartily

to it, although I receive it, it may speedily fade away and be forgotten. I must give it time to become fixed and rooted in me, to become united and identified with me by private meditation. Christians, give yourselves, give your Lord time to transfer His heavenly thoughts to your inner life. When you have read a portion, set yourselves in silence before God. Take time to remain before Him until He has made His word living and powerful in your souls. Then it will become the life and the power of your life (LT, 7-8).

This present book is designed to help you do just what Murray suggested. I've prepared this book to help us celebrate the Lord's Table in a way that will honor the Lord. I never again want to go to the Lord's Table without sensing an awesome nearness and communion with my Savior. I want to participate in a worthy manner that will draw me near to Him and bring Him pleasure in my worship.

If we will properly examine ourselves and participate in a worthy manner, the Lord's Table can be for us a time of renewing the New Covenant with our Lord. It will be a time to return to our first love. It will be a time for dealing with sin that has crept into our lives and relationships. Every observance will be another invitation to reconcile any broken relationships in the Body of Christ. The result will be a clean and pure church that loves and faithfully obeys her Lord until the day comes when we will sit down as a pure bride at the marriage supper of the Lamb. Such a clean church will be far more fruitful in obeying the final command of the Lord to expand His Kingdom by making disciples of the nations.

Use this book as your guide for personal preparation. Use it as a guide for personal cleansing. Focus your attention on the wounded Savior and the high price He paid for your forgiveness. Rekindle your memories of His blessed life and return to your first love for Him.

May you present your life as a worthy and living sacrifice to Him. May He fill you with a new sense of wonder at His love for you. I pray that this book will help your church as you join in sacred assembly and prepare the Bride of Christ for her marriage to the Lamb. Then may this clean Body and Bride of Christ fulfill the final command of our Lord by making disciples of all the nations.

➥ **As you begin your preparations, pray and ask the Lord to focus your attention on the cross and the sacrifice of His Son Jesus for your sins. Ask Him to guide you in your preparations so that you will be a worthy guest at the Supper. Don't conclude today's lesson without taking time to pray.**

Day 2
THE LAST SUPPER

Let me take you on a mental journey back in time. Go with me to Jerusalem the day before Jesus died on the cross. Jerusalem is filled with people who have come to celebrate a great festival—the Passover and the Feast of Unleavened Bread. People crowd the streets. Worshipers chant psalms of praise as they remember the miraculous way God brought Israel out of Egypt. An elder from each family or group takes a young lamb to the temple. After three loud blasts from the silver trumpets, the lambs are killed. Some blood from each lamb is sprinkled at the altar. Then the elders head home to roast their Passover lambs for the evening meal.

Peter and John are there. They are preparing for Jesus to celebrate the Passover with His twelve disciples. In an upper room a table is set with bitter herbs, unleavened bread, and four cups of wine. The roasted lamb is brought to the table as the twelve disciples gather with Jesus. Little do the disciples know that this will be the last Passover meal they will eat with their Master.

➡ **Read Luke's account of the Last Supper below and answer the questions that follow.**

When the hour came, Jesus and his apostles reclined at the table. And he said to them, "I have eagerly desired to eat this Passover with you before I suffer. For I tell you, I will not eat it again until it finds fulfillment in the kingdom of God."

After taking the cup, he gave thanks and said, "Take this and divide it among you. For I tell you I will not drink again of the fruit of the vine until the kingdom of God comes."

And he took bread, gave thanks and broke it, and gave it to them, saying, "This is my body given for you; do this in remembrance of me."

In the same way, after the supper he took the cup, saying, "This cup is the new covenant in my blood, which is poured out for you" (Luke 22:14-20).

Q1. When will Jesus eat another meal and drink of the "fruit of the vine" with His disciples?

Q2. What does the bread of the supper represent?

Q3. What does the cup (wine or juice) represent?

Jesus will eat the next meal and drink of the fruit of the vine when God's kingdom comes—when it reaches its fulfillment. The bread represents the body of the Lord that was broken on the cross for us. In a similar way the wine represents His blood that was shed for us. It is the blood of a New Covenant between God and His people.

The original Passover meal was a time to remember God's deliverance of Israel out of bondage in Egypt. The Lord's Supper was established by the Lord Jesus as a time to remember Him and His sacrifice to deliver people from their sins. He said, "do this in remembrance of me."

The day following the Last Supper, Jesus went to the cross to give His body and blood as a sacrifice for the sins of the world.

➥ **Pause to remember Jesus and His sacrifice on the cross of Calvary. Read or sing "At the Cross" by Isaac Watts.**

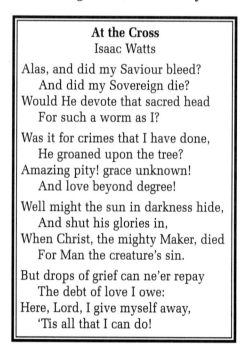

At the Cross
Isaac Watts

Alas, and did my Saviour bleed?
   And did my Sovereign die?
Would He devote that sacred head
   For such a worm as I?

Was it for crimes that I have done,
   He groaned upon the tree?
Amazing pity! grace unknown!
   And love beyond degree!

Well might the sun in darkness hide,
   And shut his glories in,
When Christ, the mighty Maker, died
   For Man the creature's sin.

But drops of grief can ne'er repay
   The debt of love I owe:
Here, Lord, I give myself away,
   'Tis all that I can do!

On that Good Friday Jesus gave His life as "the Lamb of God who takes away the sin of the world." By His payment of a death penalty for my sins and yours, we are now set free from bondage to sin. Your celebration of the Lord's Table as a sacred assembly will be a time to remember Jesus and His loving sacrifice for you.

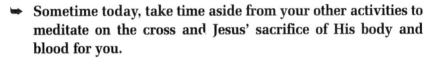 **Express your love and thanks to Jesus in prayer. Ask Him to help you remember Him in a worthy way. Write a few words of your prayer of thanksgiving on the lines below. If you prefer, write a poem of gratitude to Him.**

_____

_____

_____

_____

_____

_____

_____

_____

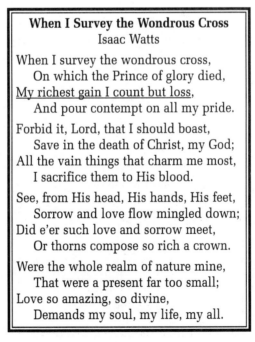 **Sometime today, take time aside from your other activities to meditate on the cross and Jesus' sacrifice of His body and blood for you.**

When I Survey the Wondrous Cross
Isaac Watts

When I survey the wondrous cross,
　On which the Prince of glory died,
My richest gain I count but loss,
　And pour contempt on all my pride.

Forbid it, Lord, that I should boast,
　Save in the death of Christ, my God;
All the vain things that charm me most,
　I sacrifice them to His blood.

See, from His head, His hands, His feet,
　Sorrow and love flow mingled down;
Did e'er such love and sorrow meet,
　Or thorns compose so rich a crown.

Were the whole realm of nature mine,
　That were a present far too small;
Love so amazing, so divine,
　Demands my soul, my life, my all.

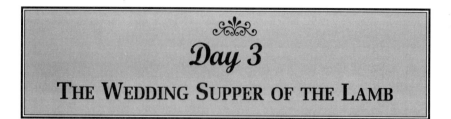

Day 3
THE WEDDING SUPPER OF THE LAMB

In Leviticus 23 God prescribed festivals and celebrations as sacred assemblies for His people. Each one had divine purposes to rekindle the love and reverence of God's people for Him. In writing to the church, Paul said that Israel's religious festivals, New Moon celebrations, and Sabbaths were "a *shadow* of the things that were to come; the reality, however, is found in Christ" (Col. 2:16-17).

For instance, some believe that Jesus was actually born during the Feast of Tabernacles when shepherds were more likely to be out in the fields at night. If this was the case, just as Israel celebrated God's coming to dwell in a Tabernacle in the days of Moses, Jesus came to live among us as Immanuel—"God with us." The feast was a shadow of the reality that was in Christ. Others believe the fulfillment of Tabernacles will come with the kingdom rule of Christ in eternity. Whenever the fulfillment takes place, we can rejoice in the reality that Christ came to dwell among us and now is in us by His Holy Spirit.

At the time of the Feast of Passover, Jesus became the Lamb of God who was slain to take away the sin of the world. Christ's sacrifice became the ultimate reality of deliverance for God's people. At Pentecost (Feast of First Fruits) the Holy Spirit came upon the disciples and the first fruits of the church were harvested as 3,000 came to faith in Christ in a single day. The fulfillment of the Feast of Trumpets will be the Second Coming of Jesus when the final trumpet will sound and call the elect home to heaven. The Day of Atonement is a shadow of Judgment Day where we all will appear before the judgment seat of Christ. Each "shadow" points to a reality in Christ.

➥ **Match the sacred assembly ("shadow") on the left with the fulfillment ("reality") on the right. Write a letter beside the number.**

___ 1. Feast of Passover	a. Judgment Day
___ 2. Feast of Pentecost	b. Birth of Jesus as Immanuel
___ 3. Feast of Trumpets	c. Death of Jesus as Lamb of God
___ 4. Day of Atonement	d. First Fruits of the Church
___ 5. Feast of Tabernacles	e. Second Coming of Christ

(Answers: 1-c; 2-d; 3-e; 4-a; 5-b) These sacred assemblies were shadows of a reality found in Christ. In a similar way the Lord's Supper is a shadow of something to come—the wedding supper of the Lamb!

➥ **Read about the wedding supper of the Lamb and underline the words or phrase that describe the preparations of the church—the Bride of Christ. What will she have done?**

> Let us rejoice and be glad and give him glory! For the wedding of the Lamb has come, and his bride has made herself ready. Fine linen, bright and clean, was given her to wear." (Fine linen stands for the righteous acts of the saints.)
>
> Then the angel said to me, "Write: 'Blessed are those who are invited to the wedding supper of the Lamb!'" (Rev. 19:7-9).

The bride already will have "<u>made herself ready</u>." She will be clean and dressed in fine linen—"the righteous acts of the saints."

➥ **Based upon your knowledge of the Christian church at large (all God's redeemed people), would you say that the Bride of Christ is clean, dressed, and ready for the wedding supper of the Lamb? Is she clean and pure? ❑ Yes ❑ No Why or why not?**_____

_____

Probably most Christians sadly would have to admit that the Bride of Christ is far from ready. She is too impure, unclean, and unrighteous to be an acceptable bride for God's only Son Jesus. The bride, however, needs to be ready for His return at any time.

Do you remember how Jesus said He would not eat the Passover or drink the fruit of the vine again until they find fulfillment in the kingdom of God (Luke 22:16, 18)? The wedding supper of the Lamb *is* that fulfillment in the coming kingdom of God. What a special day that will be for the Bride of Christ—the church. The angel said: "Blessed are those who are invited to the wedding supper of the Lamb!"

The Lord's Table is not just a time to look back at the cross. It is a time to look forward to the Lord's return for His bride. Paul said, "Whenever you eat this bread and drink this cup, you proclaim the Lord's death *until he comes*" (1 Cor. 11:26). As you prepare for the celebration of the Lord's Table, you will look back to remember the cross. You also will want to prepare yourself to be ready for your future as the pure Bride of Christ.

By looking back at the Last Supper and the Cross, you will grow in your love and appreciation of Christ for the sacrifice He made for you on the Cross. By looking forward, you will realize you need to get ready for the wedding supper of the Lamb.

As Christ's bride, we want to be clean and pleasing to Him. The Lord's Table provides a regular opportunity to prepare ourselves. We need to be right with God and each other. We need to be clean and pure. We need to be dressed in the righteous acts of the saints.

➡ **How would you describe your attention and preparations for the return of Christ and the wedding supper of the Lamb? Check one that best describes you.**

    ❑ a. I think about His return regularly and seek to keep myself clean and pure for that day. I want to be ready.

    ❑ b. I really don't think much about His return. I'm not ready.

    ❑ c. I'm somewhere between "a" and "b."

➡ **Read or sing the following song text and reflect on what a Savior we have. Think about meeting this glorious King.**

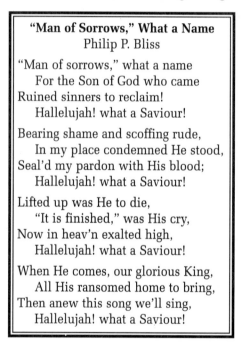

> **"Man of Sorrows," What a Name**
> Philip P. Bliss
>
> "Man of sorrows," what a name
>   For the Son of God who came
> Ruined sinners to reclaim!
>   Hallelujah! what a Saviour!
>
> Bearing shame and scoffing rude,
>   In my place condemned He stood,
> Seal'd my pardon with His blood;
>   Hallelujah! what a Saviour!
>
> Lifted up was He to die,
>   "It is finished," was His cry,
> Now in heav'n exalted high,
>   Hallelujah! what a Saviour!
>
> When He comes, our glorious King,
>   All His ransomed home to bring,
> Then anew this song we'll sing,
>   Hallelujah! what a Saviour!

➡ **Imagine what the wedding supper of the Lamb will be like. Meditate upon what kind of bride will be pleasing to Jesus. Ask the Lord to begin revealing to you anything you need to do to get your life in line with Him and His will. As the Lord begins revealing these things, take the actions needed.**

Day 4
THE DIVINE INVITATION

In Matthew 22:1-14 Jesus told a parable about His coming kingdom. A parable is a simple story that reveals spiritual truth. Jesus described a king who invited people to the wedding banquet for his son. "Tell those who have been invited that I have prepared my dinner... and everything is ready. Come to the wedding banquet" (Matt. 22:4). Sadly, those who were first invited refused to come. The king in the parable sent his army to destroy them and burn their city. What a tragedy.

Next the king sent his servants to invite anyone they could find:

> "The wedding banquet is ready, but those I invited did not deserve to come. Go to the street corners and invite to the banquet anyone you find." So the servants went out into the streets and gathered all the people they could find, both good and bad, and the wedding hall was filled with guests (Matt. 22:8-10).

The Wedding Supper of the Lamb is what we see illustrated in the parable. God is preparing a great wedding banquet for His Son Jesus Christ. He is inviting people to come. Those who come to faith in Jesus as Savior and Lord will be welcomed guests.

➡ **Read the following invitations and circle the word *come* each time it occurs.**

Matthew 11:28-30—"Come to me, all you who are weary and burdened, and I will give you rest. Take my yoke upon you and learn from me, for I am gentle and humble in heart, and you will find rest for your souls. For my yoke is easy and my burden is light."

Mark 8:34-35—Then he called the crowd to him along with his disciples and said: "If anyone would come after me, he must deny himself and take up his cross and follow me. For whoever wants to save his life will lose it, but whoever loses his life for me and for the gospel will save it."

Mark 1:14-15—Jesus went into Galilee, proclaiming the

good news of God. "The time has come," he said. "The kingdom of God is near. Repent and believe the good news!"

Revelation 22:17—The Spirit and the bride say, "Come!" And let him who hears say, "Come!" Whoever is thirsty, let him come; and whoever wishes, let him take the free gift of the water of life.

John 7:37-38—Jesus stood and said in a loud voice, "If anyone is thirsty, let him come to me and drink. Whoever believes in me, as the Scripture has said, streams of living water will flow from within him."

Each person has a choice about coming to the Lord and attending His wedding feast. Have you made plans to attend? Have you placed your faith in Jesus and what He has provided for you through His death on the cross?

➡ **Have you "come" to Jesus for His living water? Have you received the free gift of eternal life?** ❑ Yes ❑ No ❑ Not yet.

Those who have said yes to Jesus' invitation are invited to the marriage supper in eternity. As we look forward to that event, we celebrate the Lord's Table in remembrance of Him. If you have made the spiritual preparations, you are invited to the Lord's Table. Symbolically God sends the word to us: "Tell those who have been invited that I have prepared my dinner... and everything is ready. Come to the wedding banquet" (Matt. 22:4). For His children—the disciples of Jesus Christ—God has a similar invitation to the Lord's Table. He invites you to come and be nourished as you remember Jesus until He comes again.

➡ **As you read the following meditation by Andrew Murray, think about the glorious fact that you are invited to dine at the table of your Lord Jesus Christ.**

Let the King of Heaven and Earth say to you, "Come to the wedding banquet." In honor of His Son He has prepared a great supper. He has invited you to the great festival of His Divine love. He is prepared to receive and honor you as a guest and friend. He will feed you with His heavenly food.

O my brothers and sisters, you also have received this heavenly invitation. You have been asked to eat with the King of Glory! Embrace and be occupied with this honor.

Glorious invitation! I think of the banquet itself and what it has cost the great God to prepare it. To prepare for man upon this accursed earth a banquet of heavenly food—that cost Him much. That cost Him the life and blood of His Son to take away the curse and to open up to them the right and the access to heavenly blessings. Nothing less than the body and the blood of the Son of God could give life to lost men. Take time to ponder the wonders of this royal banquet.

I think of the invitation. It is as free, as wide as it could be, "without money and without price." The poorest and the most unworthy are called to it. It is an urgent and loving invitation. Not less cordial is the love which invites to it, the love which longs after sinners and takes delight in entertaining and blessing them.

I think of the blessing of the banquet. The dying are fed with the power of a heavenly life. The lost are restored to their places in the Father's house. And those that thirst after God are satisfied with God Himself and with His love.

Glorious invitation! With adoration I receive it, and prepare myself to make use of it. I have read of those who hold themselves excused because they are hindered, —one by his merchandise, another by his work, and a third by his domestic happiness. I have heard the voice which has said, "I say unto you, that none of these men which were invited shall taste of My supper." Because He who invites me is the Holy One, who will not suffer Himself to be mocked, I will prepare myself to lay aside all thoughtlessness, to withdraw myself from the seductions of the world; and with all earnestness to yield obedience to the voice of the heavenly love. I will remain in quiet meditation and in fellowship with the children of God, to keep myself free from all needless anxiety about the world, and as an invited guest, to meet my God with real hunger and quiet joy. He Himself will not withhold from me His help in this work (*LT*, 15-18).

➡ **Have you ever before stopped to think this seriously about God's invitation for you to come to Communion with Him?** ❏ Yes ❏ No

➡ **How would you describe your previous invitations to the Lord's Table? Check any that apply to your past experience.**

❏ a. I've never stopped to think that God Himself is inviting me to the Lord's Table.

❏ b. I've been awed many times by the realization that the Creator of the universe has invited me to His banquet.

❏ c. I just thought of the Lord's Table as a church event to which I was invited if I wanted to come.

❏ d. Sometimes I've chosen not to attend because I had a conflict in my schedule. I didn't think very seriously about it.

➡ **With such a wonderful invitation, do you need to cancel other plans so you can participate in this very special sacred assembly of your church?** ❏ Yes ❏ No

➥ **If so, what do you need to do?** _____

_____

_____

If you have a conflict, consider very seriously whether you cannot rearrange your schedule so you can be present with the rest of your church family for this sacred assembly.

➥ **Conclude today's lesson by reading (and praying) the following prayer by Andrew Murray. As you pray, underline statements or thoughts that are especially meaningful to you.**

Prayer

Eternal God, I have received the good tidings that there is room also for me at the table of Your Son. O God of all grace, with grateful thanks I receive Your invitation. I hunger for Your bread, O Lord. My soul thirsts for God. My flesh and my heart cry out for the Living God. When will I enter and appear before the face of God?

Lord, graciously bestow upon me this next week a real blessing in the way of preparation. Let the sight of my sinfulness humble me deeply and take away from me all hope in myself. Let the sight of Your grace again encourage me and fill me with confidence and gladness. Stir up within me a mighty desire for the Bridegroom, for the precious Jesus, without whom there could be no feast. And may I be filled with the thought that I have an invitation to eat bread in the house of my God with his only-begotten and well-beloved Son. Lord, grant this for Jesus' sake.

Lord Jesus, You have taught me: "God is a spirit, and they that worship Him must worship Him in spirit and in truth." Lord, spiritual worship I cannot bring: but You will bestow Your Spirit upon me. I entreat You, Lord, to grant the working of the Spirit. The blessing of the Supper is a high spiritual blessing. There at the Supper, the invisible God will come very near to us. Only the spiritual mind can enjoy the spiritual blessing. You know how deeply I fail in this receptiveness for a full blessing. But grant, I pray You, that the Holy Spirit may this week dwell and work in me with special power. I will surrender myself for this end to Him and to His guidance, in order that He may overcome in me the spirit of the world and renew my inner life to inherit from my God a new blessing. Lord, let Your Spirit work mightily within me.

And as I thus pray for myself, I pray also for the whole congregation. Grant, Lord, in behalf of all Your children an overflowing outpouring of Your Spirit, in order that this Supper may really be for all of us a time of quickening and renewal of our energies. Amen (*LT*, 18-20).

Day 5

From Supper to the Cross

Lead Me to Calvary
Jennie Evelyn Hussey

King of my life I crown Thee now—Thine shall the glory be;
   Lest I forget Thy thorn-crowned brow, Lead me to Calvary.

Chorus
Lest I forget Gethsemane, Lest I forget Thine agony,
   Lest I forget Thy love for me, Lead me to Calvary.

Show me the tomb where Thou wast laid, Tenderly mourned and wept;
   Angels in robes of light arrayed Guarded Thee whilst Thou slept.

Let me like Mary, thru the gloom, Come with a gift for Thee;
   Show to me now the empty tomb—Lead me to Calvary.

May I be willing, Lord, to bear Daily my cross for Thee;
   Even Thy cup of grief to share—Thou has borne all for me.

"Lest I forget Gethsemane, Lest I forget Thine agony, Lest I forget Thy love for me, Lead me to Calvary." So we will remember Him, let's follow Jesus to Calvary.

➡ **Pause to pray and ask God to help you remember Jesus and His suffering on the cross. Write a brief prayer below:**
Dear Jesus, _____

_____

_____

When Jesus had finished the Last Supper with His disciples, He began a very determined movement toward the cross. First, Jesus crossed the valley and went to the Mount of Olives to a garden area to pray. This prayer time in Gethsemane is where Jesus received the strength for the final move to the cross. Facing His own greatest temptation, Jesus said to Peter, James, and John, "'My soul is overwhelmed with sorrow to the point of death. Stay here and keep watch with me'" (Matt. 26:38). Then three times Jesus prayed,

"Father, if you are willing, take this cup from me; yet not my will, but yours be done." An angel from heaven appeared to him and strengthened him. And being in anguish, he prayed more earnestly, and his sweat was like drops of blood falling to the ground (Luke 22:42-44).

➡ **Which of the following feelings and emotions do you think Jesus must have felt? Check all you think apply.**
❑ fear of the pain from the beating, thorns, and the nails
❑ fear of the abuse, ridicule, and shame He would endure
❑ betrayal by Judas and the religious leaders of God's people
❑ sorrow and grief for those who would reject Him and His salvation
❑ hurt and disappointment due to Peter's denials—one of His closest disciples
❑ loneliness due to the desertion of the other disciples
❑ isolation from His Father when Jesus would become sin for the world
❑ wonder whether He could humanly endure to the end
❑ questions about what it would be like to carry the weight of the sins of the world in His own sinless life
❑ love for His Father that prompted Him to obey
❑ love for a lost world knowing that without Him they had no hope, but by His death they could receive salvation
❑ confidence in His Father's resurrection power
❑ eagerness to return to heaven

You may think of others. I think that all of these are possible emotions Jesus may have felt that night as He agonized in prayer.

Were You There?
Negro Spiritual

Were you there when they crucified my Lord?
  Were you there when they crucified my Lord?
Oh! Sometimes it causes me to tremble, tremble, tremble...
  Were you there when they crucified my Lord?

➡ **Read Luke 22:63–23:49 below describing the trial and crucifixion of Jesus. As you read, try to imagine that you were there in the crowd watching these events take place. Keep in mind that Jesus was the sinless Son of God who came to provide salvation to all. Think about the suffering, ridicule, and shame He endured to provide for your salvation.**

Luke 22:63–23:49

The men who were guarding Jesus began mocking and beating him. They blindfolded him and demanded, "Prophesy! Who hit you?" And they said many other insulting things to him.

At daybreak the council of the elders of the people, both the chief priests and teachers of the law, met together, and Jesus was led before them. "If you are the Christ," they said, "tell us."

Jesus answered, "If I tell you, you will not believe me, and if I asked you, you would not answer. But from now on, the Son of Man will be seated at the right hand of the mighty God."

They all asked, "Are you then the Son of God?"

He replied, "You are right in saying I am."

Then they said, "Why do we need any more testimony? We have heard it from his own lips."

Then the whole assembly rose and led him off to Pilate. And they began to accuse him, saying, "We have found this man subverting our nation. He opposes payment of taxes to Caesar and claims to be Christ, a king."

So Pilate asked Jesus, "Are you the king of the Jews?"

"Yes, it is as you say," Jesus replied.

Then Pilate announced to the chief priests and the crowd, "I find no basis for a charge against this man."

But they insisted, "He stirs up the people all over Judea by his teaching. He started in Galilee and has come all the way here."

On hearing this, Pilate asked if the man was a Galilean. When he learned that Jesus was under Herod's jurisdiction, he sent him to Herod, who was also in Jerusalem at that time.

When Herod saw Jesus, he was greatly pleased, because for a long time he had been wanting to see him. From what he had heard about him, he hoped to see him perform some miracle. He plied him with many questions, but Jesus gave him no answer. The chief priests and the teachers of the law were standing there, vehemently accusing him. Then Herod and his soldiers ridiculed and mocked him. Dressing him in an elegant robe, they sent him back to Pilate....

Pilate called together the chief priests, the rulers and the people, and said to them, "You brought me this man as one who was inciting the people to rebellion. I have examined him in your presence and have found no basis for your charges against him. Neither has Herod, for he sent him back to us; as you can see, he has done nothing to deserve death. Therefore,

I will punish him and then release him."

With one voice they cried out, "Away with this man! Release Barabbas to us!" (Barabbas had been thrown into prison for an insurrection in the city, and for murder.)

Wanting to release Jesus, Pilate appealed to them again. But they kept shouting, "Crucify him! Crucify him!"

For the third time he spoke to them: "Why? What crime has this man committed? I have found in him no grounds for the death penalty. Therefore I will have him punished and then release him."

But with loud shouts they insistently demanded that he be crucified, and their shouts prevailed. So Pilate decided to grant their demand. He released the man who had been thrown into prison for insurrection and murder, the one they asked for, and surrendered Jesus to their will.

As they led him away, they seized Simon from Cyrene, who was on his way in from the country, and put the cross on him and made him carry it behind Jesus. A large number of people followed him, including women who mourned and wailed for him. Jesus turned and said to them, "Daughters of Jerusalem, do not weep for me; weep for yourselves and for your children....

For if men do these things when the tree is green, what will happen when it is dry?"

Two other men, both criminals, were also led out with him to be executed. When they came to the place called the Skull, there they crucified him, along with the criminals— one on his right, the other on his left. Jesus said, "Father, forgive them, for they do not know what they are doing." And they divided up his clothes by casting lots.

The people stood watching, and the rulers even sneered at him. They said, "He saved others; let him save himself if he is the Christ of God, the Chosen One."

The soldiers also came up and mocked him. They offered him wine vinegar and said, "If you are the king of the Jews, save yourself."

There was a written notice above him, which read: THIS IS THE KING OF THE JEWS.

One of the criminals who hung there hurled insults at him: "Aren't you the Christ? Save yourself and us!"

But the other criminal rebuked him. "Don't you fear God," he said, "since you are under the same sentence? We are punished justly, for we are getting what our deeds deserve. But this man has done nothing wrong."

Then he said, "Jesus, remember me when you come into your kingdom."

Jesus answered him, "I tell you the truth, today you will be with me in paradise."

It was now about the sixth hour, and darkness came over the whole land until the ninth hour, for the sun stopped shining. And the curtain of the temple was torn in two. Jesus called out with a loud voice, "Father, into your hands I commit my spirit." When he had said this, he breathed his last.

The centurion, seeing what had happened, praised God and said, "Surely this was a righteous man." When all the people who had gathered to witness this sight saw what took place, they beat their breasts and went away. But all those who knew him, including the women who had followed him from Galilee, stood at a distance, watching these things.

➡ **On the lines below, write out a prayer of thanksgiving to Jesus for the ridicule, shame, suffering, and death He endured for you. If you prefer, write it in the form of a poem or a song.**

Day 6
BROKEN BODY AND SHED BLOOD

The Lord's Table provides a powerful symbol of the sacrifice Jesus made to provide for our forgiveness. Let's reflect on the broken body and shed blood symbolized in the bread and wine.

> The Lord Jesus, on the night he was betrayed, took bread, and when he had given thanks, he broke it and said, "This is my body, which is for you; do this in remembrance of me." In the same way, after supper he took the cup, saying, "This cup is the new covenant in my blood; do this, whenever you drink it, in remembrance of me." For whenever you eat this bread and drink this cup, you proclaim the Lord's death until he comes (1 Cor. 11:23-26).

Matthew records these words and actions of Jesus:

> Jesus took bread, gave thanks and broke it, and gave it to his disciples, saying, "Take and eat; this is my body."
> Then he took the cup, gave thanks and offered it to them, saying, "Drink from it, all of you. This is my blood of the covenant, which is poured out for many for the forgiveness of sins" (Matt. 26:26-28).

➥ **Read the following Scriptures that describe what Christ did for us through His blood. In each verse underline what Jesus has done through His blood. I've underlined the first one for you.**

> "Be shepherds of the <u>church of God, which he bought</u> with his own blood" (Acts 20:28).

> "Since we have now been justified by his blood, how much more shall we be saved from God's wrath through him!" (Rom. 5:9).

> "To him who loves us and has freed us from our sins by his blood..." (Rev. 1: 5).

"How much more, then, will the blood of Christ... cleanse our consciences from acts that lead to death, so that we may serve the living God!" (Heb. 9:14).

"For God was pleased to have all his fullness dwell in him, and through him to reconcile to himself all things... by making peace through his blood, shed on the cross" (Col. 1:19-20).

"But now in Christ Jesus you who once were far away have been brought near through the blood of Christ" (Eph. 2:13).

"If we walk in the light, as he is in the light, we have fellowship with one another, and the blood of Jesus, his Son, purifies us from every sin" (1 John 1:7).

Oh what Jesus accomplished by His blood: (1) He bought the church. (2) He justified us. (3) He freed us from our sins. (4) He cleanses our consciences from acts that lead to death. (5) He made peace between God and us. (6) He brought us near. (7) He purifies us from all sin.

➡ **Read or sing the following hymn and meditate on the power in the blood shed for you. Underline the things that can be accomplished because of the power in the blood of Christ shed for you. I've underlined one for you.**

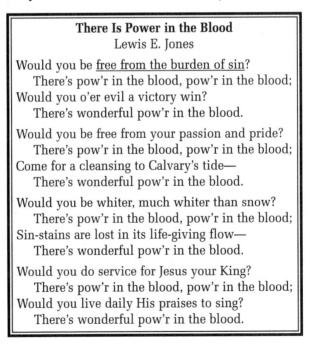

There Is Power in the Blood
Lewis E. Jones

Would you be <u>free from the burden of sin</u>?
  There's pow'r in the blood, pow'r in the blood;
Would you o'er evil a victory win?
  There's wonderful pow'r in the blood.

Would you be free from your passion and pride?
  There's pow'r in the blood, pow'r in the blood;
Come for a cleansing to Calvary's tide—
  There's wonderful pow'r in the blood.

Would you be whiter, much whiter than snow?
  There's pow'r in the blood, pow'r in the blood;
Sin-stains are lost in its life-giving flow—
  There's wonderful pow'r in the blood.

Would you do service for Jesus your King?
  There's pow'r in the blood, pow'r in the blood;
Would you live daily His praises to sing?
  There's wonderful pow'r in the blood.

Now, I'm going to guide you through an activity that may seem rather childish. I want to ask you to humble yourself and do it anyway. One person approached this assignment and started not to do it because of its simplicity. But he finally decided to cooperate with me. He spoke to me later and told me how it had a far greater impact on him than he expected. By the time he got to the Lord's Table, the meaning of Christ's shed blood had taken on a much deeper meaning. Take just a moment to be like a child again.

➡ **To help you more clearly understand the suffering of the Lord, I want you to draw the blood on the following picture of Christ. If one is available, get a red pen or crayon. Draw the blood...**
- on his head where the crown of thorns was placed
- on his hands and feet where the nails were driven
- on his sides and shoulders where the whips on his back drew blood
- on his side where the spear was placed to see if he was dead
- on the ground where the blood fell

➡ In a sense Jesus speaks to us from the cross, saying "I loved you this much!" Take a few minutes in prayer to thank Him for His love and the sacrifice of His life for you, for shedding His blood for you. Tell Him how much you love Him for what He has done. If you prefer, write a brief statement to Him of your love.

_____

_____

_____

_____

_____

_____

➡ Now close by reading or singing the following hymn. Spiritually open yourself to receive the cleansing Christ can give.

Are You Washed in the Blood?
Elisha A. Hoffman

Have you been to Jesus for the cleansing pow'r?
   Are you washed in the blood of the Lamb?
Are you fully trusting in His grace this hour?
   Are you washed in the blood of the Lamb?

Are you walking daily by the Savior's side?
   Are you washed in the blood of the Lamb?
Do you rest each moment in the Crucified?
   Are you washed in the blood of the Lamb?

When the Bridegroom cometh will your robes be white?
   Are you washed in the blood of the Lamb?
Will your soul be ready for the mansions bright
   And be washed in the blood of the Lamb?

Lay aside the garments that are stained with sin
   And be washed in the blood of the Lamb;
There's a fountain flowing for the soul unclean,
   O be washed in the blood of the Lamb!

Chorus
Are you washed in the blood,
   In the soul-cleansing blood of the Lamb?
Are your garments spotless? Are they white as snow?
   Are you washed in the blood of the Lamb?

Day 7
THE WOUNDED SAVIOR

When Jesus was born in Bethlehem an angel appeared to some shepherds and proclaimed: "'I bring you good news of great joy that will be for all the people. Today in the town of David a **Savior** has been born to you; he is Christ the Lord'" (Luke 2:10-11). Jesus came to be our Savior. He came to save people from their sins (Matt. 1:21). But because of our sin and God's justice, the only way our salvation could be purchased was by the shedding of His blood: "without the shedding of blood there is no forgiveness" (Heb. 9:22). Jesus was the Lamb of God who takes away the sin of the world. His life was the perfect sacrifice and sufficient sacrifice for our sins. Jesus had to die on the cross to be our Savior.

➥ **Turn back one page and look again at the picture of Jesus on the cross. Begin today's lesson by reflecting on the wounded Savior on the cross. Pray and thank the Lord Jesus for giving His life so that you could be forgiven. Thank Him for the suffering He endured. Tell Him how much you love Him.**

Jesus demonstrated a great love for you and for me on that cross.

➥ **How would you describe the love you feel for Jesus right now? Check the one that best describes your love. If these responses are not adequate, write one of your own.**
  - ❑ a. I'm humbled and moved to tears to think that Jesus loved a sinner like me that much.
  - ❑ b. I know He loved me in my head, but I'm still having trouble feeling that love in my heart.
  - ❑ c. I wish He were physically present so I could give Him a hug.
  - ❑ d. Even with the knowledge that Jesus did all that for me, somehow, I still don't sense that love in a real way.
  - ❑ e. Other: _____
    _____
    _____
    _____

I would guess that people could respond in any one of the ways I've suggested above. When we really grasp the price Jesus paid to be our Savior, words can never express adequately the love we should have for Him. I pray that you will come to a deep, real, and personal experience of the love of Christ. Perhaps through this study and your experience at the Lord's Table, Jesus Himself clearly will reveal His love to you so that you experientially will know that you are deeply loved by your Savior. Lord Jesus, make it so.

Eight hundred years before Christ, Isaiah described the suffering Servant and the price He would pay to save us from our sins.

➥ **Read the Isaiah 53:3-12 below and underline words or phrases that describe the suffering and abuse Jesus endured to be your Savior. I've underlined a couple for you.**

He is <u>despised and rejected</u> of men; a man of sorrows, and acquainted with grief: and we hid as it were our faces from him; he was despised, and we esteemed him not.

Surely he hath borne our griefs, and carried our sorrows: yet we did esteem him stricken, smitten of God, and afflicted. But <u>he was wounded</u> for our transgressions, he was bruised for our iniquities: the chastisement of our peace was upon him; and with his stripes we are healed. All we like sheep have gone astray; we have turned every one to his own way; and the Lord hath laid on him the iniquity of us all. He was oppressed, and he was afflicted, yet he opened not his mouth: he is brought as a lamb to the slaughter, and as a sheep before her shearers is dumb, so he openeth not his mouth....

Yet it pleased the LORD to bruise him; he hath put him to grief: when thou shalt make his soul an offering for sin, he shall see his seed, he shall prolong his days, and the pleasure of the LORD shall prosper in his hand. He shall see of the travail of his soul, and shall be satisfied: by his knowledge shall my righteous servant justify many; for he shall bear their iniquities. Therefore will I divide him a portion with the great, and he shall divide the spoil with the strong; because he hath poured out his soul unto death: and he was numbered with the transgressors; and he bare the sin of many, and made intercession for the transgressors (Isa. 53:3-12).

Despised, rejected, filled with sorrows, familiar with suffering, unesteemed, carried our infirmities and sorrows, stricken, smitten, afflicted, pierced crushed, punished, wounded, oppressed, led to the slaughter like a lamb, cut off from the living, caused to suffer by God's will, poured out His life, numbered with transgressors, and bore our sins—all that Jesus did for you because of His great love, His unbelievable love.

➡ **In the following song written by Frances Havergal, Jesus asks some questions. As you read (or sing) this song, underline the four questions.**

> ### I Gave My Life for Thee
> Frances R. Havergal
>
> I gave My life for thee,
>   My precious blood I shed,
> That thou might'st ransomed be,
>   And quickened from the dead
> I gave, I gave My life for thee—
>   What hast thou giv'n for Me?
>
> My Father's house of light,
>   My glory-circled throne
> I left, for earthly night,
>   For wand'rings sad and lone;
> I left, I left it all for thee—
>   Hast thou left aught for Me?
>
> I suffered much for thee,
>   More than thy tongue can tell,
> Of bitt'rest agony,
>   To rescue thee from hell;
> I've borne, I've borne it all for thee—
>   What hast thou borne for Me?
>
> And I have brought to thee,
>   Down from My home above,
> Salvation full and free,
>   My pardon and My love;
> I bring, I bring rich gifts to thee—
>   What hast thou brought to Me?

A Testimony of the Moravian Brethren

In *The Key to the Missionary Problem* (New York: American Tract Society, 1901) Andrew Murray describes a moving encounter with Christ that Count Nicholas Ludwig von Zinzendorf had in a Dusseldorf museum. A painter named Sternberg had painted a picture of the suffering Christ. Sternberg himself had been so affected by the love of Christ for him, that he wanted to do something for Christ. He wanted to paint a picture of Jesus that would convey His love. Below the picture Sternberg wrote the words: "All this I did for thee, What hast thou done for Me?" (This probably was the inspiration for the song you just read.) Here's a description of what happened to Zinzendorf:

> His heart was touched. He felt as if he could not answer the question. He turned away more determined than ever to spend his life in the service of his Lord. The vision of that Face never left him. Christ's love became the constraining power of his life. "I have," he exclaimed, "but one passion— 'tis He, and He only." It was His dying love that fitted Christ for the work God had given Him as the Saviour of men. It was the dying love of Christ mastering his life that fitted Zinzendorf for the work he had to do (*Missionary Problem*, 45).

➥ **Have you ever experienced God's love so fully that love for Jesus Christ was your one passion? Take a moment to pray and ask the Lord to stir up your passion for the suffering Savior.**

Zinzendorf returned to his estate to provide spiritual leadership for a group called the Moravians. About 300 people had moved to his estate to escape religious persecution. Most were Moravians (a religious group related to the martyr John Hus). But the refugees included Lutherans, followers of Calvin and Zwingli, Anabaptists, and others. In the Spring of 1727 internal conflict was about to destroy the religious community. Zinzendorf and three others drew up a covenant of brotherly union that described the way these Christians would live together. It recognized their differences, but insisted on brotherly love and unity in the Body of Christ.

On May 12, 1727, the entire community repented of their divisions, were reconciled with their brethren, and entered into a covenant to live in harmony to honor their Lord. Murray quoted from their diary account of that day:

> The Brethren all promised, one by one, that they would be the Saviour's true followers. Self-will, self-love, disobedience—they bade these farewell. They would seek to be poor in spirit; no one was to seek his own profit before that of others; everyone would give himself to be taught by the Holy Spirit (*Missionary Problem*, 47).

God began to bind this body of believers together in love and unity. On August 13, 1727, they had a significant encounter with their Savior at a Lord's Supper observance. I want you to read their story as a faith builder for your own church's upcoming Supper.

On Sunday, 10th, Pastor Rothe was leading the afternoon meeting at Herrnhut, when he was overpowered and fell on his face before God. The whole congregation bowed under the sense of God's presence, and continued in prayer till midnight. He invited the congregation to the Holy Supper on the next Wednesday, the 13th.

As it was the first communion since the new fellowship, it was resolved to be specially strict with it, and to make use of it "to lead the souls deeper into the death of Christ, into which they had been baptized." The leaders visited every member, seeking in great love to lead them to true heart-searching. In the evening of Tuesday, at the preparation service, several passed from death to life, and the whole community was deeply touched.

"On the Wednesday morning all went to Berthelsdorf. On the way thither, any who had felt estranged from each other afresh bound themselves together. During the singing of the first hymn a wicked man was powerfully convicted. The presentation of the new communicants touched every heart, and when the hymn was sung it could hardly be recognized whether there was more singing or weeping. Several brethren prayed, specially pleading that, as exiles out of the house of bondage, they knew not what to do, that they desired to be kept free from separation and sectarianism, and besought the Lord to reveal to them the true nature of His Church, so that they might walk unspotted before Him, might not abide alone but be made fruitful. We asked that we might do nothing contrary to the oath of loyalty we had taken to Him, nor in the very least sin against His law of love. We asked that He would keep us in the saving power of His grace, and not allow a single soul to be drawn away to itself and its own merits from that Blood-and-Cross Theology, on which our salvation depends. We celebrated the Lord's Supper with hearts at once bowed down and lifted up. We went home, each of us in great measure lifted up beyond himself, spending this and the following days in great quiet and peace, and learning to love."

Among those present in the church when the communion was held were a number of children. One writes: "I cannot attribute the great revival among the children to anything else but that wonderful outpouring of the Holy Spirit on the communion assembly. The Spirit breathed in power on old and young. Everywhere they were heard, sometimes at night in the field, beseeching the Saviour to pardon their sins and make them His own. The Spirit of grace had indeed been poured out" (*Missionary Problem*, 49-50).

Following that encounter with Christ at the Lord's Table, the Moravian Brethren carried a zeal for missions. They began a 24-hour prayer watch for the causes of Christ's kingdom that continued uncnding for ovor ono hundred years. During the following twenty years they sent out over 100 missionaries.

Some of those missionaries met John Wesley on a boat headed for America. In them Wesley saw a personal faith in Christ, a love for Christ, and a calm assurance that was different than his own. He returned to London. In a Moravian chapel at Aldersgate, Wesley came to a personal faith in Christ. He went from there a different man and led the evangelical revival (First Great Awakening) in England. Even William Carey (known as the Father of Modern Missions) was greatly influenced toward missions by the testimonies of Moravian missionaries.

In *The Key to the Missionary Problem* Murray quoted Rev. P. de Schweinitz who summed up the work of the Moravian Brethren.

➡ **As you read this description of Moravian missions, look for the thing that motivated and inspired their work. Underline their "battle-cry."**

> "Even today [1900] the Moravians have for every fifty-eight communicants in the home churches a missionary in the foreign field, and for every member in the home churches they have more than two members in the congregation gathered from among the heathen. . . . Now, what was the incentive for foreign missionary work which has produced such results? While acknowledging, the supreme authority of the great commission, the Moravian Brethren have ever emphasized as their chief incentive the inspiring truth drawn from Isaiah 53:10-12: making our Lord's suffering the spur to all their activity. From that prophecy they drew their missionary battle-cry: 'To win for the Lamb that was slain, the reward of His sufferings.' We feel that we must compensate Him in some way for the awful sufferings which He endured in working out our salvation. The only way we can reward Him is by bringing souls to Him. When we bring Him souls, that is compensation for the travail of His soul. In no other way can we so effectively bring the suffering Saviour the reward of His passion as by missionary labour, whether we go ourselves or enable others to go. Get this burning thought of 'personal love for the Saviour who redeemed me' into the hearts of all Christians, and you have the most powerful incentive that can be had for missionary effort. Oh, if we could make this missionary problem a personal one! if we could fill the hearts of the people with a personal love for this Saviour who died for them,

the indifference of Christendom would disappear, and the kingdom of Christ would appear." (*Missionary Problem*, 36-37).

➡ **Copy the battle-cry of the Moravians below.**

_____

_____

➡ **Which of the following best describes the thought that motivated and inspired the Moravians to serve Christ? Check one.**
   ❏ a. They read the commands of Christ and served out of a sense of duty to the commands.
   ❏ b. Their spiritual leaders like Zinzendorf made them feel guilty and ashamed if they did not serve.
   ❏ c. Their love for the wounded Savior who died to redeem them gave them a zeal to serve the Lord.

Oh that we might see Christ as our wounded Savior in the same way. These men and women were prepared to give their all, even their lives, because of the love of Christ. Paul described this motivation this way:

> Christ's love compels us, because we are convinced that one died for all, and therefore all died. And he died for all, that those who live should no longer live for themselves but for him who died for them and was raised again (2 Cor. 5:14-15).

At a picture gallery in Germany, God instilled in Count Zinzendorf a personal love for the wounded and suffering Savior. His life and ministry were forever changed as he resigned from his governmental duties to work with God's people on his estate. At the Lord's Table those Moravian Brethren had a moving encounter with the wounded Savior, and they were never the same. I pray that the upcoming Lord's Table experience will be just as moving for you and your church.

By the way, I wondered about that painting of Jesus in Dusseldorf. I would like to see a painting of my Lord that so significantly inspired Zinzendorf and many others. The painting was destroyed in a fire, so we have nothing left but the testimonies of those who were changed by an encounter with the living Christ. Let's allow our heart-love for the indwelling Christ to be sufficient.

➡ **Close by praying that God will give you and those in your church a deeper love for your wounded Savior than you have ever known before. Listen this next few weeks to the question, "All this I did for you. What have you done for me?"**

Week 2

Preparations to Partake in a Worthy Manner

"Whoever eats the bread or drinks the cup of the Lord in an unworthy manner will be guilty of sinning against the body and blood of the Lord. A man ought to examine himself before he eats of the bread and drinks of the cup."

Overview of Week 2

Day 1: Examine Yourself
Day 2: Judge Yourself
Day 3: Remove Idols of the Heart
Day 4: Consecrate Your Home
Day 5: Reconcile and Forgive
Day 6: Humble Yourself in Servanthood
Day 7: Pre-Communion Meditations

This week you will begin to prepare yourself to partake of the Lord's Table in a worthy manner. As you plan your week, you may want to keep the following things in mind. On Day 4 you will be asked to schedule time with your family (if they live in your home and if they also are preparing for the Lord's Table). Plan for a time when you can complete this assignment prior to the Lord's Table—even if you do it earlier in the week. If your church has a pre-Communion meeting scheduled, please prepare to attend.

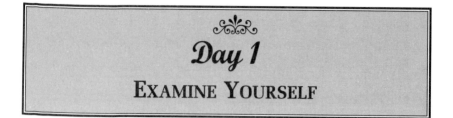

Day 1

EXAMINE YOURSELF

Paul wrote to the Corinthian church about the Lord's Table. He sent a word of correction because they were partaking of the supper in an unworthy manner. As we prepare for the Supper, we need to follow Paul's instructions so that we will be acceptable guests at the Lord's Table.

➡ **Read Paul's instructions for self-examination. <u>Underline what Paul had to say about the consequences of eating in an unworthy manner and bringing judgment upon yourself. What had happened to many among the church?</u>**

> Therefore, whoever eats the bread or drinks the cup of the Lord in an unworthy manner will be guilty of sinning against the body and blood of the Lord. A man ought to examine himself before he eats of the bread and drinks of the cup. For anyone who eats and drinks without recognizing the body of the Lord eats and drinks judgment on himself. That is why many among you are weak and sick, and a number of you have fallen asleep. But if we judged ourselves, we would not come under judgment. When we are judged by the Lord, we are being disciplined so that we will not be condemned with the world (1 Cor. 11:27-32).

Paul explained the danger of partaking in an unworthy manner. Some were weak and sick and others had died (fallen asleep). He went on to explain that we can either judge ourselves, or we can come under the Lord's judgment. This is one of the reasons I've prepared this book for you. I don't want you to go the way of the Corinthians and treat the Lord's Table casually. I don't want you to suffer the consequences of the Lord's discipline and judgment. To avoid that, you need to examine yourself. You need to treat the Lord's Table seriously and be prepared to partake in a worthy manner.

The first step of examination is to ask yourself, am I in the faith? Paul wrote to the Corinthians: "Examine yourselves to see whether you are in the faith; test yourselves. Do you not realize that Christ

Jesus is in you—unless, of course, you fail the test?" (2 Cor. 13:5). How would you know for sure whether you are "in the faith"? Paul said you would know it by the Spirit of Jesus Christ that is in you.

➡ **Read the following Scriptures and underline the words that describe ways a person can know he or she is "in the faith." I've underlined the first one for you.**

> **Romans 8:16**—<u>The Spirit himself testifies</u> with our spirit that we are God's children.
>
> **1 John 2:3-6**—We know that we have come to know him if we obey his commands. The man who says, "I know him," but does not do what he commands is a liar, and the truth is not in him. But if anyone obeys his word, God's love is truly made complete in him. This is how we know we are in him: Whoever claims to live in him must walk as Jesus did.
>
> **1 John 3:24**—Those who obey his commands live in him, and he in them. And this is how we know that he lives in us: We know it by the Spirit he gave us.
>
> **1 John 4:13**—We know that we live in him and he in us, because he has given us of his Spirit.

The Holy Spirit testifies (or bears witness) to your spirit that you belong to God. The presence and work of the Holy Spirit in you can help you know you are God's child. John says you can know you are in Him if you obey His commands.

➡ **Does the Holy Spirit bear witness to you that you are a child of God?** ❏ Yes ❏ No ❏ I just don't know for sure.

➡ **Do you obey Christ and walk as Jesus walked in such a way that you know the Spirit of Christ dwells in you?**
❏ Yes ❏ No ❏ My inconsistency raises questions for me.

➡ **Have you placed your faith and trust in Jesus Christ alone for your salvation?** ❏ Yes ❏ No

➡ **If you have that relationship with Jesus Christ, take a moment to reflect on the time when you entered into that saving relationship with Him. Write below some of your memories of that time.**

_____

_____

_____

Only those who have been genuinely converted by Jesus Christ and have entered into a saving relationship with Him are worthy guests at the Lord's Table. You are worthy because of what Christ has done in you, not because of your own righteousness or goodness.

Last week we looked at a parable Jesus told about the wedding banquet and those who were invited. When those who had been invited to the banquet refused to come, the King sent his servants out into the streets to invite everyone they could find to the banquet. But...

> "When the king came in to see the guests, he noticed a man there who was not wearing wedding clothes. 'Friend,' he asked, 'how did you get in here without wedding clothes?' The man was speechless.
>
> "Then the king told the attendants, 'Tie him hand and foot, and throw him outside, into the darkness, where there will be weeping and gnashing of teeth'" (Matt. 22:11-13)

Those who don't have a saving faith relationship with Jesus Christ, are not prepared for the Wedding Supper with the Lamb. They are not wearing the proper "wedding garment." Since the Lord's Table is a time to remember what Jesus did for you in providing for your salvation, this relationship with Him is a vital part of being a worthy guest. If you have not yet turned to Jesus in saving faith, you should not participate in the Lord's Table. If you have questions about your relationship with Jesus Christ, you have help:

> The Spirit himself testifies with our spirit that we are God's children. (Rom. 8:16).

➡ **Read the following meditation by Andrew Murray (from his book *The Lord's Table*). Ask God's Holy Spirit to reveal to you the truth about your saving relationship with Jesus Christ. Pray before you begin reading.**

Andrew Murray's Meditation on Self-Examination

The problem of self-examination is simple. According to the apostle, there are but two conditions, either Jesus Christ is in you, or ye are reprobate [rejected]: one of two. There is no third condition. The life of Christ in you may still be weak; but if you are truly born again and a child of God, Christ is in you. And then as a child you have access to the table of the Father and a share in the children's bread.

But if Christ is not in you, you are rejected. Nothing that is in you, nothing that you do, or are, or even desire and wish to be, makes you acceptable to God. The God against whom you have sinned inquires only about one thing: whether you have received His Son. "He that has the Son has the life." If Christ is in you, you are acceptable to the Father. But if Christ is not in you, you are at the very same moment rejected. You have come in to the Lord's Supper without the wedding garment: your lot must be in the outermost darkness. You are unworthy. You eat judgment to yourself. You make yourself "guilty of the body and blood of the Lord."

Reader, how is it with you? What will God say of you when He sees you at the table? Will God look upon you as one of His children, who are very heartily welcome to Him at His table, or as an intruder who has no right to be at His table? Reader, What will God say of you when He beholds you at His table? You are one of two things: you are either a true believer and a child of God, or you are not. If you are a child of God, you have a right to the table and to eat the bread of the Father, however feeble you may be. But if you are not a child of God—no true believer—you have no right to it. You may not go forward to it.

Examine your own self. Are you in the faith? Test yourself. Should it appear that you do not yet have Christ in you, then even today you can receive Him. There is still time. Without delay give yourself to Christ: in Him you have a right to the Lord's Table! (*LT*, 32-35).

Next Andrew Murray offers two prayers. One is for all to pray, asking God to reveal the true condition of their hearts before Him. The other is for those who are not yet in the faith—those who realize that Jesus does not live in them yet.

➡ **Read through the first prayer, and let it become your prayer. Pray it to the Lord.**

Prayer for All

"Search me, O God, and know my heart, try me and know my thoughts, and see if there is any wicked way in me and lead me in the way that is everlasting." Lord, You know how deceitful the heart is. It is deceitful far above all things. But, Lord, You know the heart, even my heart. Now I come to You, All-Knowing One. I set my heart before You with this prayer: Lord, make me know whether Jesus Christ is in me, or whether I am still without Him and rejected before You.

You, Yourself, saw to it that hypocrites should be cast out from the midst of Your people. You pointed out Achan. You made known Judas who dipped his hand in the dish with Your Son. You are the King who scrutinized the guests and cast out the one without a wedding garment. You are still mighty to search the hearts. Lord, hear now the prayer of Your people, and purge Your congregation. Let the life of the Spirit become so powerful that all doubts shall vanish.

Help Your children to know and confess that Christ is in them. Let Your presence in our midst effect such a joy and such a reverence that those who merely confess Christ with their lips will be afraid. Permit the self-righteous to be revealed. Lord, make it known to many who are still content in uncertainty, whether Christ is in them or whether they are reprobate and rejected.

Great God, make this known to me: Is Jesus Christ in me? Let the Holy Spirit give me the blessed assurance of this. Then I will sit down with confidence as Your child at Your table.

And if Jesus Christ is still not in me, and I am still without Christ and rejected before You, make this known to me. Make me willing to know this. Give me a reverence so I'll not draw near to Your table except that Jesus Christ is in me. Amen (*LT*, 35-37).

➥ **As you have placed yourself before God seeking to know if you are His child, what do you sense His Spirit has revealed to you? Check the one that best describes your condition.**
  ❑ a. Jesus is in me. I know it by the witness of His Spirit in me.
  ❑ b. My life in Christ is very weak, but Jesus is in me.
  ❑ c. I am still without Christ. He is not in me.
  ❑ d. I still am not sure which of these conditions is true of me.

If you checked *a* or *b* jump down to the closing activity of the lesson. If you still are not sure about your condition before God (*d*), continue to seek His counsel. We have time. God wants you to know more than you desire it, so continue to seek Him. If doubt persists, go ahead and settle your relationship with Him in faith. If you realize that you are still without Christ (*c*), move to the next prayer activity below.

➥ **If you checked *c* or *d*: Read the following prayer by Andrew Murray for those who realize that Christ is not in them. If you agree with the prayer, receive Jesus Christ as your Savior.**

Prayer for One Without Christ

Lord God, I had thought of going forward to Your table. A sense of obligation came even to me, and I made myself ready for the hour of the feast. But, behold, Your word has made me afraid. It tells me that, if Jesus Christ is not in me, I am an unworthy guest.

Lord, have compassion upon me. I know that I may not sit down without the wedding garment. You are Lord of the table. Your word must prevail there. You are the Holy God. You cannot meet in love with the sinner who is not washed from his sin and clothed with the righteousness of Christ. Lord, I fear that I am still without that wedding garment: my sins are not forgiven. Lord, have pity upon me. I dare not go to Your table. The bread of Your children is not for me.

I dare not go forward. And yet, Lord, I dare not remain away. To have no part in Jesus, no share in Your friendship, no place in the Marriage Supper of the Lamb on high—woe is me. Lord, have mercy upon me. Grant to me what I need for sitting down at Your table.

Lord God, I have heard of Your mercy. You give the wedding garment as a free gift. You forgive the worst sinner. Too long have I been content without really having Jesus Christ in me. Lord, now I come to You. I lay my unrighteousness before You. I am entirely under the power of sin, and cannot help myself. Lord, You alone can help me. Please receive me. I cast myself down here before You: I surrender myself to You. This day, let the blood of Jesus wash me and make me clean.

Lord Jesus, given by the Father for me, I receive You. I receive You, Lord, as my Savior. I believe that You are for me. Here I give You my heart—my poor, sinful heart. Come and dwell in it, and let me also know that Jesus Christ is in me.

My God, my soul cries out and longs for You: make me truly a partaker of Jesus Christ. Amen (*LT*, 37-39).

➡ **If you have prayed to receive Christ just now, contact your pastor to share the good news. Who else do you need to tell?**

➡ **Close your devotional period today by reflecting on the joy of those who have been redeemed by saving faith in Jesus Christ.**

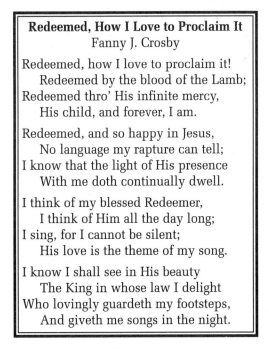

Redeemed, How I Love to Proclaim It
Fanny J. Crosby

Redeemed, how I love to proclaim it!
　　Redeemed by the blood of the Lamb;
Redeemed thro' His infinite mercy,
　　His child, and forever, I am.

Redeemed, and so happy in Jesus,
　　No language my rapture can tell;
I know that the light of His presence
　　With me doth continually dwell.

I think of my blessed Redeemer,
　　I think of Him all the day long;
I sing, for I cannot be silent;
　　His love is the theme of my song.

I know I shall see in His beauty
　　The King in whose law I delight
Who lovingly guardeth my footsteps,
　　And giveth me songs in the night.

Day 2
JUDGE YOURSELF

Today, we continue to prepare ourselves to be worthy guests at the Lord's Table. Not only do you need to examine yourself to see if you are in the faith, but you also need to examine yourself to see if you are clean from sin. God gives you a choice. You can either judge yourself and thoroughly repent of your sin. Or you can hold on to your sin and come under God's judgment and discipline.

➥ **Read again what Paul wrote to the Corinthians. Circle the words *judged* and *judgment*. Then answer the questions that follow.**

Therefore, whoever eats the bread or drinks the cup of the Lord in an unworthy manner will be guilty of sinning against the body and blood of the Lord. A man ought to examine himself before he eats of the bread and drinks of the cup. For anyone who eats and drinks without recognizing the body of the Lord eats and drinks judgment on himself. That is why many among you are weak and sick, and a number of you have fallen asleep. But if we judged ourselves, we would not come under judgment. When we are judged by the Lord, we are being disciplined so that we will not be condemned with the world (1 Cor. 11:27-32).

➥ **Q1. If you judge yourself, what will you avoid?**

_____

Q2. Why does God judge or discipline His people?

_____

_____

➥ **Using the passage above, fill in the blanks that describe ways God may have disciplined Christians for not taking the body of the Lord seriously.**
"That is why many among you are _____ and _____, and a number of you have

_____   _____."

If you judge yourself, you will not come under God's judgment. When God does judge or discipline you, He does it so you will not be condemned with the world. Some of the Corinthians had experienced God's discipline in physical ways: they were weak, sick, or had fallen asleep (died).

➠ **Based on this truth, which of the following would you rather do? Check one.**

❑ a. I would rather judge myself, repent of sin, and be right with God.

❑ b. I would rather hold on to my sinful ways and ignore or treat casually the fact that Christ's body was broken for me. I'll take my chances of being disciplined by God.

I assume that you would probably choose *a*. However, if you checked *b*, that indicates that you do not have a healthy reverence for a holy God.

➠ **Read what God has to say about the way we deal with our sins through the writer of Proverbs. Then answer the questions that follow.**

He who conceals his sins does not prosper, but whoever confesses and renounces them finds mercy. Blessed is the man who always fears the Lord, but he who hardens his heart falls into trouble (Pro. 28:13-14).

➠ **Q1. What does a person find when he or she confesses and renounces personal sin?** _____

Q2. What happens to a person who hardens his heart toward God and hides or conceals his sin?

_____

_____

Q3. What is the condition of a person "who always fears the Lord"? _____

When you confess and renounce (quit) your sin, you find mercy from God. He forgives and cleanses you from sin. You do this because you have a healthy fear and reverence for your holy God. The person who covers and tries to hide his sin will not prosper. In fact he or she "falls into trouble." You cannot hide your sin from God. He loves you too much to leave you in an unworthy life and in the gutter with sin. Out of His love for you, God will discipline you.

"My son, do not make light of the Lord's discipline, and do not lose heart when he rebukes you, because the Lord disciplines those he loves, and he punishes everyone he accepts as a son" (Heb. 12:5-6).

God disciplines you because He loves you too much to let you continue living below the abundant life Jesus died to give you.

➡ **Read the following Scriptures that tell how we should deal with sin. After each Scripture is one or more statements. Mark each statement T (true) or F (false) by circling T or F.**

I preached that they should repent and turn to God and prove their repentance by their deeds (Acts 26:20).

➡ **T – F 1. I prove my repentance by what I *say*, not what I *do*.**

If we walk in the light, as he is in the light, we have fellowship with one another, and the blood of Jesus, his Son, purifies us from all sin.

If we claim to be without sin, we deceive ourselves and the truth is not in us. If we confess our sins, he is faithful and just and will forgive us our sins and purify us from all unrighteousness. If we claim we have not sinned, we make him out to be a liar and his word has no place in our lives (1 John 1:7-10).

➡ **T – F 2. If I confess my sin, God will forgive and purify me.**

Nevertheless, God's solid foundation stands firm, sealed with this inscription: "The Lord knows those who are his," and, "Everyone who confesses the name of the Lord must turn away from wickedness" (2 Tim. 2:19).

➡ **T – F 3. I can truthfully claim that Jesus is my Lord and live a wicked life at the same time.**

This is the verdict: Light has come into the world, but men loved darkness instead of light because their deeds were evil. Everyone who does evil hates the light, and will not come into the light for fear that his deeds will be exposed. But whoever lives by the truth comes into the light" (John 3:19-21).

➡ **T – F 4. People who are Christians should try to cover up their sin as if nothing is wrong.**

T – F 5. People who do evil tend to hide from God's light so that their evil deeds will not be exposed.

(Answers: True: 2, 5; False: 1, 3, 4). If you live by God's truth, you will voluntarily come into the light and get rid of your sin. Trying to hide your sin indicates that Jesus is not really your Lord as you may claim. You need to agree with God about (confess) your sin and turn away from wickedness. When you do, God forgives, cleanses, and restores you to right fellowship with Himself. God offers you a wonderful invitation: "'Come now, let us reason together,' says the LORD. "Though your sins are like scarlet, they shall be as white as snow; though they are red as crimson, they shall be like wool" (Isa. 1:18).

I want to encourage you to judge yourself before coming to the Lord's Table. The Holy Spirit who lives in you has the job assignment of convicting you of sin. He will assist you in examining your life to see if there is any sin which you need to confess and renounce.

➥ **Pray the prayer of the Psalmist below and ask the Lord to reveal to you any area of sin that you have not confessed and turned away from your wicked deeds.**

Search me, O God, and know my heart; test me and know my anxious thoughts. See if there is any offensive way in me, and lead me in the way everlasting (Ps. 139:23-24).

➥ **Prayerfully read through the following list of sins and areas of sin. Ask the Lord to reveal to you any area in which you have not turned away from sin and experienced His cleansing. Ask Him to show you any sin that is hindering your fellowship with Him. You may want to check any that God identifies, so you can deal with your sin seriously. You may prefer to write these on a separate sheet of paper that can be disposed of later.**
❏ unbelief—not believing God will keep His word
❏ rebellion—disobedience, not letting Christ be Lord of all, living my own way
❏ pride/arrogance—thinking more highly of myself than I ought, more than what God knows to be true of me
❏ bitterness, unforgiveness, holding a grudge
❏ sins of the tongue—gossip, slander, murmuring, lying, cursing, filthy speech, vain talk, obscenity
❏ dishonesty, deceit
❏ mental impurity, filthy thought life
❏ addiction to harmful or illegal substances
❏ addiction to pornography (either visual or written)
❏ sexual immorality

- ❏ stealing, cheating, embezzlement
- ❏ anger, hatred, malice, rage, uncontrolled temper
- ❏ idolatry—worshipping another god, or loving something or someone more than I love God
- ❏ poor stewardship of my time and resources
- ❏ prayerlessness
- ❏ taking unfair advantage of others, oppressing others
- ❏ disobedience to the clear commands of the Lord
- ❏ injustice, failing to defend the oppressed
- ❏ murder, hating my brother without a cause
- ❏ causing strife, conflict, and dissension in the church
- ❏ worshipping with my lips when my heart is far away from loving the Lord
- ❏ leaving my first love for Christ by loving other people, things, or activities more than the Lord
- ❏ Others_____

This is certainly not a complete list of sins. You can miss God's standards in many ways through your thoughts, actions, and words. Develop a heart that is ready to confess and repent at the slightest whisper of conviction from the Holy Spirit. If God has convicted you of sin, take action now to get right with Him.

- Confess: agree with God that you have sinned.
- Repent: turn away from your sin and turn to God to live His way.
- Seek the Lord's forgiveness and cleansing.
- Show your repentance by a changed life/deeds.

Here's what God does with your sin when you confess and repent:

> Let the wicked forsake his way and the evil man his thoughts. Let him turn to the Lord, and he will have mercy on him, and to our God, for he will freely pardon (Isa. 55:7).

> "I, even I, am he who blots out your transgressions, for my own sake, and remembers your sins no more" (Isa. 43:25).

> You will again have compassion on us; you will tread our sins underfoot and hurl all our iniquities into the depths of the sea (Mic. 7:19).

➡ **Talk to the Lord about any sin He has revealed. Judge yourself. Confess your sin and repent. Thank Him for His forgiveness and cleansing. Pledge to live His way and for His glory.**

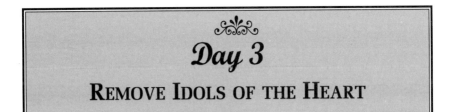

Day 3
REMOVE IDOLS OF THE HEART

God spoke to Ezekiel about the elders in Israel: "'These men have set up idols in their hearts and put wicked stumbling blocks before their faces'" (Ezek. 14:3). Jesus said the first and greatest commandment is this: "'Love the Lord your God with all your heart and with all your soul and with all your mind'" (Matt. 22:37). Anything that takes the place of your first love for God can be a false god or an "idol of the heart."

Leaving your first love for God by turning to an "idol of the heart" can be a serious matter. In His message to the church at Ephesus in Revelation 2, Jesus told the church the consequences if they did not return to their first love.

➡ **Read Revelation 2:4-5 below and underline the phrase that describes what Jesus said he would do if they did not repent and return to their first love for Christ.**

"I hold this against you: You have forsaken your first love. Remember the height from which you have fallen! Repent and do the things you did at first. If you do not repent, I will come to you and remove your lampstand [church] from its place" (Rev. 2:4-5).

Jesus said He would remove the church from its place if they did not return to their first love for Him. Violating the first and greatest commandment is serious with God. An idol of the heart is anything that captures your love and attention in a way that keeps you from your first love for Him. Let's look at some of those things.

➡ **In each of the following Scriptures circle the word or phrase that describes something that can get in the way of your first love for God or that can be an idol of the heart.**

"No one can serve two masters. Either he will hate the one and love the other, or he will be devoted to the one and despise the other. You cannot serve both God and Money" (Matt. 6:24).

Do not love the world or anything in the world. If anyone

loves the world, the love of the Father is not in him (1 John 2:15).

Can you imagine how dangerous this matter is for many Christians and churches today? Love of <u>money</u>, the <u>world</u>, or any <u>thing</u> in the world prevents you from loving God fully. The materialism of many Christians is a major idol of the heart that they may not even realize. How about you?

➠ **If you were honest before God, how would you rate your love for money and things? Check one that is most like you or write your own.**

❑ a. I'm obsessed with the love of money and things. Much of my life revolves around seeking after money for what it can secure for me or in buying and enjoying things that are beyond the basic necessities of life.

❑ b. I probably love things too much. If I had to choose between my things and loving the Lord fully, I might be tempted to waver.

❑ c. I don't have much in the way of material things, but I'd have to confess that my desires for those things are far too strong.

❑ d. Though I seek to have a first love for the Lord, sometimes I realize that my things are too important to me.

❑ e. God has led me to choose Him over my money and things on several occasions, and I'm growing more and more fully in love with Him.

❑ f. Other: _____

➠ **If you realize that you may have idols in your heart, confess your sin to the Lord. Ask Him to help you identify the idols. Ask Him to help you return to your first love for Him.**

Jacob's Family Assembly

Jacob returned to the Promised Land after being away for years building a family. He became afraid of the people of the land and said, "We are few in number, and if they join forces against me and attack me, I and my household will be destroyed" (Gen. 34:30). When Jacob was in distress, God told him to return to Bethel for a time of worship. Bethel is where God had met him years before when Jacob was running away from his brother Esau. There God had entered into the covenant with Jacob that He had established with Abraham and Isaac before him. Now God was preparing to renew His covenant promises with Jacob and his sons. Jacob knew his family needed to get ready to meet with a holy God.

➤ **As you read the description of this family's sacred assembly, look for the things Jacob's family did to get ready to meet with God at Bethel.**

> Jacob said to his household and to all who were with him, "Get rid of the foreign gods you have with you, and purify yourselves and change your clothes. Then come, let us go up to Bethel, where I will build an altar to God, who answered me in the day of my distress and who has been with me wherever I have gone." So they gave Jacob all the foreign gods they had and the rings in their ears, and Jacob buried them under the oak at Shechem. Then they set out, and the terror of God fell upon the towns all around them so that no one pursued them (Gen. 35:2-5).

➤ **What did Jacob's family do to prepare to meet with God?**

_____

_____

Jacob consecrated his family and had them put away their foreign gods and the impurities they had accumulated. They even changed clothes to be physically clean before the Lord. God responded by causing the people of the land to fear God and stay away from Jacob and his family. Then at Bethel, Jacob's family had a wonderful worship experience and God renewed His covenant with Jacob and gave him a new name—Israel (see Gen. 35:6-15).

As you look forward to meeting with God at the Lord's Table, you need to examine your heart and your household goods to see if you have any false gods or idols of the heart that you need to deal with.

➤ **Ask the Lord to reveal any "idols of the heart" that may have led you away from your wholehearted love for the Lord. These may be things that are not evil in themselves, but they have captured too much of your love. You may not need to throw these away, but you may need to give them away or sell them to break their hold on your love. Only the Lord can reveal to you whether something has captured your love like that. He will also help you understand what you must do to break their ties to your heart.**

Ask God to help you. One way you might test something is to ask yourself, "If God, Himself, asked me to give this up, would I resist Him or have a struggle to do it?" If you are holding on too tightly, the item may be an "idol of the heart." These things could include:

- Hobbies or collections (the idol may be things or activities)
- A material object that you treasure too dearly
- Material things that consume far too much of your time using them or maintaining them
- Things you have to impress others or that cause you to feel arrogant or condescending toward others
- Things you have purchased for yourself that you know God didn't want you to have
- Activities you love that consume too much of your time and may even keep you from your time with God or from serving Him obediently

➡ **Make a list of the things or activities God brings to your mind. If you have questions about whether an item has become an idol in your heart, talk to the Lord about it until you have peace about God's assessment. If something comes to mind and you still are not sure about whether it is an idol in your heart, write it down with a question mark. Continue praying about the matter until you have some clear direction from the Lord. Use extra paper if you need space.**

_____

_____

_____

_____

_____

I used to collect Indian arrowheads. I treasured them. I wouldn't sell them even when I received a good offer because of my love for them. At one point, I came to realize they had become idols in my heart. I came to the conviction that I had to get rid of them to break the hold they had on my heart.

I found a business owner of a rock shop who said he would buy them from me. I made the long trip to his shop ready to sell my entire collection. He looked at them and decided they were not the quality he wanted. He said he did not care to buy them. I was disappointed as I made the trip back home.

Then I remembered God's dealing with Abraham and his son Isaac. Once Abraham proved his willingness to obey God and give Isaac as a sacrifice, God gave Isaac back to his father. (See Gen. 22:1-18.) Once I had given my arrowheads to the Lord by agreeing to sell them, their hold on my heart was broken. Later I did find a buyer for some of them and I sold some of my best ones just to make sure their hold on me was gone. Then I gave the money to a Christian ministry to make sure my motives were pure.

If you realize that you have a heart idol, pray and ask the Lord what to do with it. I don't know what He may ask you to do. You may need to throw it away, destroy it, give it away, sell it, or do something else to break the hold it has on your spirit. You may even need to evaluate your use of television, the Internet, or some other activity to determine whether these are heart idols. God may guide you to exercise temperance in these activities. In other cases He may ask you to quit the activity altogether. Remember that returning to your first love for Christ is serious business.

➡ **If you have identified idols of your heart pray about the following and check each one when you finish.**

❑ Confess to the Lord that you have given your love and attention to these items. Agree with Him that you have sinned.

❑ Ask Him to forgive and cleanse you.

❑ Ask Him to set you free from your love for these things. Remember the height from which you have fallen and return to Him as your first love.

❑ Pledge to Him your renewed loyalty, love, and desire to please Him and obey Him.

➡ **For the items that need to be given away or sold, make immediate plans to carry out your plan of surrender and obedience with regard to those items. Write below a note about anything God is leading you to do and check it off when you have done it. Use extra paper if you need space.**

❑ _____

_____

❑ _____

_____

❑ _____

_____

❑ _____

Day 4

CONSECRATE YOUR HOME

As you prepare to meet with God at the Lord's Table, I want you to consecrate yourself, your family, and your home for that time. In a sense, this is a time for a family "sacred assembly." If you live alone or your family doesn't know the Lord, use the following instructions in the way that will be most appropriate for you.

➡ **Prepare for a family assembly. Before the time for the Lord's Table, make plans for a family gathering. You may need to adjust your schedule to another night so everyone can be present. Place a trash can or bag in the center of the room.**

Moses Consecrated the People

When Israel had left Egypt, they came to the "Mountain of God" where Moses would be given the Ten Commandments. This event was later celebrated by the Jews during the sacred assembly on the Day of Pentecost each year. Prior to meeting with the people, the Lord announced His plans. He gave Moses these instructions:

> "Go to the people and consecrate them today and tomorrow. Have them wash their clothes and be ready by the third day, because on that day the Lord will come down on Mount Sinai in the sight of all the people...."
>
> After Moses had gone down the mountain to the people, he consecrated them, and they washed their clothes. Then he said to the people, "Prepare yourselves for the third day. Abstain from sexual relations."
>
> On the morning of the third day there was thunder and lightening, with a thick cloud over the mountain, and a loud trumpet blast. Everyone in the camp trembled. Then Moses led the people out of the camp to meet with God (Ex. 19:10-11, 14-17).

God is still a holy God, yet we have gotten to the place we are far too casual when we enter into His presence. We may have allowed many impurities of the world into our homes and lives without taking time to think how unacceptable they may be to the Lord. Or we may have failed to get rid of evil things from our old sinful life once we came to faith in Christ.

A Bonfire at Ephesus

When Paul began a church in Ephesus, God used Paul and demonstrated His power by working miracles through him. When seven Jews tried to cast out a demon "in the name of Jesus whom Paul preaches," the demon possessed man beat them severely.

➡ **Read how the Christians in Ephesus sought to get right with a holy God.**

> When this became known to the Jews and Greeks living in Ephesus, they were all seized with fear, and the name of the Lord Jesus was held in high honor. Many of those who believed now came and openly confessed their evil deeds. A number who had practiced sorcery brought their scrolls together and burned them publicly. When they calculated the value of the scrolls, the total came to fifty thousand drachmas. In this way the word of the Lord spread widely and grew in power (Acts 19:13-20).

➡ **What two things did the Ephesian Christians do?**
They openly confessed their _____
They burned their _____

When the people came to realize how holy God really is, they got rid of the unholy things in their lives—even when the action was costly. They openly confessed and turned away from their evil deeds. They burned the things related to their former practice of sorcery. The result was that the work of the Kingdom spread and grew in power.

➡ **Pray and ask God to reveal to you and your family members the things you have in your home that represent the impurities of the world that God would like for you to get rid of. Confess to the Lord that you want to be clean and pure before Him. Give Him permission to clean your home of impurities. Check here after you have prayed: ❏**

Now begin a process of consecrating your home. You may want to do a family tour of your house room-by-room. Assume that Jesus is coming to your home and He will take a careful look in every room.

He will see the things in closets and drawers. He will see the music you listen to and the videotapes you watch. He will look on the shelves at your reading literature. Nothing will escape His pure gaze.

> **What is there in your home that you would be ashamed for Jesus to see?**

These are the things that you need to throw away.

➡ **Invite family members to join in cleaning the house of the spiritual and moral impurities that may have collected there. Here is a suggestive list for you to consider. As God brings an item to mind, send a person to get it and throw it into your trash can or read the list and then walk through each room cleaning as you go. In every case let God's Holy Spirit guide your conscience. If you have doubts or disagreement about an item, pause and pray about it and ask the Lord how He thinks about it. Consider such things as:**

- Music CDs, tapes, or records with lyrics that are impure, ungodly, or unholy
- Movies, DVDs, or recorded videos that have language, images, themes, or actions that are impure or unholy—especially those that are sources of temptation toward lust, sensuality, violence, or materialism [Don't let the world's rating system be your criteria for acceptable content. What would be pleasing and acceptable to the Lord?]
- Novels, magazines, or other printed literature that is pornographic either visually or mentally
- Books that are used for false worship or that encourage ungodly behavior
- Books, clothing, or items used by fraternal organizations that are incompatible with serving and worshiping God alone
- Images, souvenirs, pictures, sculptures, paintings, and so forth that may be items of worship in false religions or that are used in the practice of witchcraft or the occult (e.g. Ouija board or a statue of a false god)
- Alcohol, drugs, tobacco, or any other substance that has become a vice to you, that is damaging to your body, or that contributes to intemperance

- Games or computer programs that have impure, wicked, ungodly, or unholy subject matter or practices; games that lead to impure physical contact or interaction between the sexes
- Clothing that you know is immodest or that was intended to be seductive
- Any other material thing that is a source of temptation to sin

➠ **Once you have collected the things that need to be disposed of, gather the family together again. Check these items as you respond to God in prayer.**
   ❑ Confess to the Lord that you have tolerated evils and impurities that are not appropriate for His holy people. Agree with Him that you have sinned.
   ❑ Ask Him to forgive and cleanse you.
   ❑ Ask Him to set you free from any desire to hold on to the impurities. Ask Him to change your heart in love and obedience to Him.
   ❑ Pledge to Him your renewed loyalty, love, and desire to please Him and obey Him.
   ❑ Thank Him for the purity He is bringing into your life.

➠ **Now dispose of your items that need to be thrown out. You may need to take them to a dumpster, burn them, or in some other way remove the temptation to go back out to the garbage can and retrieve them later. Things that are evil or impure don't need to be passed along to others either. Make sure the items are disposed of permanently.**

Day 5

RECONCILE AND FORGIVE

When Paul wrote to the Corinthians about the Lord's Supper, he expressed his concerns about the divisions in the church. Disunity in Christ's body is a serious sin.

> I hear that when you come together as a church, there are divisions among you.... When you come together, it is not the Lord's Supper you eat, for as you eat, each of you goes ahead without waiting for anybody else. One remains hungry, another gets drunk.... Do you despise the church of God and humiliate those who have nothing? What shall I say to you? Shall I praise you for this? Certainly not! (1 Cor. 11:18-22).

The church often had a meal in addition to the elements of the Lord's Supper itself. The rich neglected the poor and showed contempt for the body of Christ. Notice the other statements Paul wrote to the Corinthians regarding divisions in their church.

> I appeal to you, brothers, in the name of our Lord Jesus Christ, that all of you agree with one another so that there may be no divisions among you and that you may be perfectly united in mind and thought. (1 Cor. 1:10).

> Brothers, I could not address you as spiritual but as worldly.... For since there is jealousy and quarreling among you, are you not worldly? Are you not acting like mere men? (1 Cor. 3:1-3).

➡ **Based on this last Scripture, when there is jealousy, quarreling, or division in your church what are you acting like?**

Churches that are divided and quarreling look just like the world and mere men, not like followers of Christ. The night before Jesus went to the cross, He prayed for our unity: "'I in them and you in me. May they be brought to complete unity to let the world know that you sent me and have loved them even as you have loved me'" (John 17:23). Our unity is the most convincing evidence to the lost world that Jesus is the Savior sent from God. That also means that our disunity is probably the greatest hindrance in leading others to faith in Christ. If you have broken relationships with brothers and sisters in Christ, you must be reconciled.

➡ **Read the following statements by Jesus about the importance of right relationships between brothers (and sisters) in Christ. Underline what a person needs to do to get the relationship right.**

"When you stand praying, if you hold anything against anyone, forgive him, so that your Father in heaven may forgive you your sins" (Mark 11:25).

"If you are offering your gift at the altar and there remember that your brother has something against you, leave your gift there in front of the altar. First go and be reconciled to your brother; then come and offer your gift" (Matt. 5:23-24).

➡ **Match the conditions described in 1 and 2 below with the correct response (a, b, c, or d) below them. Write a letter beside the number.**

___ 1. If I am the offender and my brother holds a grudge against me...

___ 2. If my brother has offended me and I am holding a grudge against him...

Responses:

a. I should ignore the problem and hope it goes away.

b. I should wait until my brother takes the first step by coming to me to get things right.

c. I should immediately forgive the offense even if my brother has not asked for forgiveness.

d. I should delay my worship and be reconciled with my brother first so my worship will be acceptable.

Jesus knows the importance of right relationships in the body of Christ. He commands us to respond in a way that is directly opposite to what our human nature would suggest. If I am the offender, my worship isn't acceptable until I've been reconciled. If my brother is the offender, I should forgive him even though he may not have asked for forgiveness. That is pretty radical isn't it! But that is why unity can be such a powerful testimony to a watching world. The rest of the world doesn't act that way. (Answers: 1-d; 2-c)

➥ **Read through the following list of relationships that may need to be made right in your life. Place a check beside any item that describes a relationship you have that needs reconciliation. I've provided some space along the way for notes if you need it.**

❏ Have I mistreated anyone by my actions or with my words that I have not gone to the person and asked forgiveness?

❏ Have I stolen anything from a person, an organization, a business, my employer, or anyone else and not gone back and made restitution?

❏ Do I hold a grudge or bitterness in my heart toward anyone?

❏ Have I gossiped about or slandered another person?

❏ Have I borrowed anything that I have failed to return?

❏ Has God impressed me to do something to meet another person's needs and I have failed to obey Him?

❏ Have I done anything illegal which I need to confess?

_____

_____

❏ Have I lied to anyone or falsified information?

❏ Have I hurt someone because of an immoral act and covered it up rather than clean and clear it up?

❏ Am I currently in a wrong or immoral relationship with anyone?

❏ Have I been guilty of not expressing gratitude to a person or group when I certainly should have? Am I taking someone for granted and need to show my gratitude in words and deeds?

❏ Have I allowed jealousy, envy, or resentment to have a negative effect on the way I have related to a person or group?

❏ Have I allowed pride to keep me from relating to a person who needed a friend?

_____

_____

❏ Have I sinned against God and another person or group by committing any of the following sins?

❏ anger	❏ anxiety	❏ arguing
❏ arrogance	❏ bitterness	❏ blasphemy
❏ boasting	❏ coarse talking	❏ conceit
❏ complaining	❏ competition	❏ covetousness
❏ cursing	❏ critical spirit	❏ deception
❏ unforgiveness	❏ discord	❏ disorder
❏ divisiveness	❏ envy	❏ factions
❏ faultfinding	❏ fear	❏ fits of rage

- ❏ gossip
- ❏ greed
- ❏ grumbling
- ❏ hatred
- ❏ hypocrisy
- ❏ impatience
- ❏ impurity
- ❏ independence
- ❏ injustice
- ❏ insensitivity
- ❏ jealousy
- ❏ lack of love
- ❏ lies
- ❏ malice
- ❏ oppression
- ❏ persecution
- ❏ prejudice
- ❏ pride
- ❏ quarreling
- ❏ resentment
- ❏ revenge
- ❏ rudeness
- ❏ slander
- ❏ strife
- ❏ unbelief
- ❏ self-seeking

- ❏ judgmental spirit
- ❏ intolerance of differences
- ❏ party spirit (factions)
- ❏ lawsuits among believers
- ❏ provoking one another
- ❏ keeping record of wrongs
- ❏ self-righteousness
- ❏ a controlling spirit
- ❏ selfish ambition
- ❏ struggle for control
- ❏ spirit of superiority
- ❏ delighting in downfall of a brother

If the Holy Spirit has brought to your mind any relationships that are broken or ways you have contributed to disunity in the body of Christ, decide now to make those relationships right.

➡ **List below any persons or groups whom you have offended by your sin and need to be forgiven and reconciled.**

- ❏ _____
- ❏ _____
- ❏ _____
- ❏ _____
- ❏ _____
- ❏ _____
- ❏ _____
- ❏ _____
- ❏ _____
- ❏ _____

If You Are the Offender[1]

1. Pray and ask God for help in thorough repentance.
2. Go to make things right out of obedience to God.
3. Put the hardest person first on your list.
4. Confess your sin to God and to those directly affected by the sin.
5. Don't apologize. Ask for forgiveness.

6. Go in person (best choice), call by phone (second choice), or write a letter (last resort).
7. Don't reflect negatively on the other person or his actions or attitudes. Deal only with your part of the offense.
8. Make restitution (pay for the offense) when appropriate.
9. Don't expect to receive a positive response every time. Continue to pray for and seek reconciliation with an unforgiving person. Jesus command is: "Be reconciled."

➥ **List below any persons or groups by whom you have been offended by their sin. Include only those where you have not forgiven or where the relationship remains broken.**

❑ _____
❑ _____
❑ _____
❑ _____
❑ _____
❑ _____
❑ _____
❑ _____
❑ _____
❑ _____

If You Are the One Offended[1]

1. Forgive the offender. Forgiveness is a command, not an option: "Bear with each other and forgive whatever grievances you may have against one another. Forgive as the Lord forgave you" (Col. 3:13). "'If you do not forgive men their sins, your Father will not forgive your sins'" (Matt. 6:15).
2. You cannot forgive and love in your own strength. The Holy Spirit of Christ in you can enable you to forgive and love. Ask Him to enable you to forgive.
3. Forgiveness is a choice of your will, not the result of a feeling. You must choose to forgive.
4. Begin to pray for God to work in the person's life for his or her good. Continue praying until you can do so with a sincere desire to see God bless the person for his or her good.
5. Make an investment in the person who wronged you by returning good for evil. Ask God to guide you in this response and in the timing of it. Ask Him what you can do to meet a need or show love.

Other Teaching on Forgiveness

- Forgiveness is fully releasing another from the debt of the offense.
- The person who forgives is the one who has to pay the price of forgiveness. Jesus paid the price for you.
- You are never more like Jesus than when you forgive and show grace and mercy. Being offended provides you with the invitation to reveal Christ to the offender by your forgiveness.
- Forgiveness does not mean that the offense was not wrong.
- Forgiveness is not permission for the offender to do it again. It does not require you to place yourself in harms way again.
- Forgiveness does not mean that you will fully forget. You choose not to hold the offense against the person any longer.
- How much do you forgive? "Seventy times seven" (Matt. 18:21-22, KJV). In other words: forgive an unlimited amount.
- Jesus said, "'If [your brother] sins against you seven times in a day, and seven times comes back to you and says, "I repent," forgive him'" (Luke 17:4). In other words: even if the offender really doesn't repent and change his ways, you still forgive.
- Even if the person doesn't believe he's wrong, forgive. Jesus set the model for us on the cross when He prayed for those who were killing Him, "'Father, forgive them, for they do not know what they are doing'" (Luke 23:34).

These lists may have brought to mind too many broken relationships for you to get them all reconciled by the time of the Lord's Table. God is looking at your heart. Begin the process of reconciling relationships. God welcomes His needy children to His Table where they can be nourished and strengthened. Perhaps the experience of the Lord's love and sacrifice at the Lord's Table will strengthen you for the work of reconciliation ahead of you.

➡ **Close this lesson by praying that God would guide you to forgive and reconcile every broken relationship in a way that would bring Him glory in your life.**

➡ **Review the lists in this lesson for the offender and the offended. Underline important thoughts. On separate paper make a list of steps God is guiding you to take immediately to be reconciled and to forgive.**

---

[1]I've been influenced greatly in these matters by Life Action Ministries, P. O. Box 31, Buchanan, Michigan 49107-0031 (www.LifeAction.org). They have valuable resources to guide you in reconciling relationships.

Day 6
HUMBLE YOURSELF IN SERVANTHOOD

On the night of the Last Supper, Jesus was giving last minute lessons and instructions to His disciples. He knew clearly what they would face on the following day. He knew that His remaining days with them would be limited. He was preparing to entrust the entire future of His Kingdom into their hands. In John, chapters 13–17, Jesus gave some of His most significant messages to these followers on that night before the cross. On such a somber night and in the presence of the Lord Jesus, an unusual debate arose among the disciples.

➡ **Read how Jesus responded and answer the questions.**

A dispute arose among them as to which of them was considered to be greatest. Jesus said to them, "The kings of the Gentiles lord it over them; and those who exercise authority over them call themselves Benefactors. But you are not to be like that. Instead, the greatest among you should be like the youngest, and the one who rules like the one who serves. For who is greater, the one who is at the table or the one who serves? Is it not the one who is at the table? But I am among you as one who serves (Luke 22:24-27).

➡ **Q1. What were the disciples arguing about?**
Which of them would be the _____

Q2. How do the kings of the Gentiles relate to their subjects?

_____

Q3. How do those who call themselves Benefactors relate?

_____

Q4. What should the greatest among Christ's disciples be like?

_____

Q5. How should a disciple "rule"?

_____

Jesus the Savior, the King of kings, the Creator of the heavens and earth, the Ruler of the universe was in the room with them, and the disciples were arguing about who would be the greatest. How disoriented they were to Christ and His Kingdom work. How arrogant they were to argue about their own greatness in the presence of the King. And this was not the first time Jesus had to correct them. They had this argument at least once before (see Matt. 20:20-28). They still didn't understand.

Earthly human rulers demand that people submit to their position or to their authority. They use their power, position, or influence to "throw their weight around" and pressure others to follow. Often they act in a demanding or dictatorial manner. In a spirit of arrogance they often look down on the ones they rule as ignorant and inferior. Jesus made it clear that this was not the way to be great in His Kingdom. Greatness would come through humility and servanthood.

Jesus offered Himself as their Model: "I am among you as one who serves." On this very night after the meal, Jesus took a towel and basin of water and washed the disciples dirty feet (see John 13:2-17). He said,

> "You call me 'Teacher' and 'Lord,' and rightly so, for that is what I am. Now that I, your Lord and Teacher, have washed your feet, you also should wash one another's feet. I have set you an example that you should do as I have done for you" (John 13:13-15).

➥ **When you are in a place of leadership around God's people (at church, on a committee or board, in a class, or even in your home) which style of leadership do you tend to use? Honestly check the one that more nearly describes you. If you prefer, write a list of your own words to describe your leadership.**

❑ a. proud, arrogant, forceful, "throw my weight around," manipulative, argumentative, claim my rights, exercise authority, demanding, impatient, unyielding, uncompromising, condescending, critical

❑ b. humble, gentle, understanding, patient, cooperative, a listener, teachable, correctable, willing to lay down my rights or opinion for the sake of the Body, seek to point others to the leadership of Christ, prayerful, a servant of the Body

❑ c. Other: _____

_____

_____

_____

As I write this lesson I am grieved and distressed at the conflict in the churches I know or hear about. Division abounds. Pastors, staff, committees, boards, elders, deacons, and sometimes the entire congregation are in turmoil. Groups are polarized. Pastors and staff get fired. Angry members leave the church and sometimes in a large church split. There is very little love for one another—a love that seeks the best for the other. Often, in my observation, the issue is the same one the disciples were arguing about that night at the Supper. God's people are fighting over who will be the greatest, who will be in control, who will get to have their way, who will win. When the church of the living Christ acts in this way, we disgrace the name of Christ and bring reproach on Christ's Kingdom.

Pride is a root sin. When it is strong in your life, it can lead to or encourage other sins like: being argumentative, boastful, complaining, having a critical spirit, demanding, disobedient, exalting self, faultfinding, being a gossip, haughty, impatient, independent, showing ingratitude, being men pleasers, prejudice, rude, stubborn, unforgiving, prayerless, self-righteous, self-sufficient, having selfish ambition, self-promotion, a judgmental spirit, sexual immorality, taking a license to sin, being rebellious toward authority, desiring or demanding control, following your own evil desires, thinking more highly of self, or being unrepentant and holding on to sin.

➥ **Read what God has to say about pride. Circle the words** *pride* **and** *proud* **each time they occur.**

I hate pride and arrogance, evil behavior and perverse speech (Pro. 8:13).

Pride goes before destruction, a haughty spirit before a fall (Pro. 16:18).

I will put an end to the arrogance of the haughty and will humble the pride of the ruthless (Isa. 13:11).

The LORD preserves the faithful, but the proud he pays back in full (Ps. 21:33).

Though the LORD is on high, he looks upon the lowly, but the proud he knows from afar. (Ps. 138:6).

The LORD detests all the proud of heart. Be sure of this: They will not go unpunished (Pro. 16:5).

"God opposes the proud but gives grace to the humble." Humble yourselves, therefore, under God's mighty hand, that he may lift you up in due time (1 Peter 5:5-6).

➥ **In the last Scripture Peter gives you a way to combat pride in your life. What are you to do to yourself?**

When you humble yourself before God, He can gain glory for Himself through your life. He Himself will lift you up in due time. God tells us of another value to being humble, lowly, and contrite:

> This is what the high and lofty One says—he who lives forever, whose name is holy: "I live in a high and holy place, but also with him who is contrite and lowly in spirit, to revive the spirit of the lowly and to revive the heart of the contrite" (Isa. 57:15).

God chooses to live with those who are contrite and lowly in spirit. Those are the ones He chooses to revive. Let's humble ourselves individually and as churches corporately so that we may experience revival. The big question then becomes, How do I humble myself? Let me suggest some ways you might humble yourself. The following list describes some actions that can be humbling. Seek the Lord's direction as you choose when and how to humble yourself before God and man.

• acknowledge God's greatness and sovereignty
• give all credit and glory to Christ
• agree with God about your sin
• repent of sin
• give up or yield your rights
• lead from a position of loving service to those you lead
• lay down your plans, dreams, opinions, and preferences for those of others
• yield a position of authority to another, if God so directs
• assume the subordinate role
• serve others
• accept lowly tasks without complaint
• perform lowly tasks well
• publicly confess sin when appropriate
• confess your weaknesses or needs and accept help
• submit to those in authority over you without complaint
• fast in brokenness (secretly, don't tell anyone during or after)
• obey God even when it doesn't make sense or is costly
• yield to the desires or wishes of subordinates
• lift up others above yourself
• accept humiliating circumstances as valuable lessons

- confess dependence on God and interdependence on others
- honor others above yourself
- do the things "pride" tells you not to do
- ask critics and contenders to pray for you
- die to your self-life
- deny your selfish desires
- give away or dispose of things that cause you to feel proud
- ask for help
- express your needs
- receive help from others when you need help
- allow others to "wash your feet"
- ask others to pray for you
- place yourself before God as utterly helpless
- agree with Christ that apart from Him you can do nothing
- accept invitations to take a lowly place
- yield control to others
- give to the needy
- be willing to associate with people of low degree
- submit to one another out of reverence for Christ
- look out for the needs of others rather than your own
- surrender to God's will
- look up at the infinite God and see how small you are
- do things for others anonymously
- accept and perform menial tasks without complaint

May I offer one last word of suggestion? Pride is a sin that normally cannot be dealt with privately. The very nature of pride would encourage you to keep quiet about your pride. To refuse to confess the sin of pride to God and others may strengthen the pride in you rather than deal with it ruthlessly. Watch for opportunities (or even seek them out) where you can acknowledge your pride to a brother or sister in Christ and ask him or her to pray for you. You might have an occasion in a group setting where such a confession would be appropriate. Humility was a distinguishing mark of Jesus Christ: He "made himself nothing, taking the very nature of a servant" and "humbled himself and became obedient to death—even death on a cross!" When the humility of Christ begins to pervade your life, you will bring Him glory and honor.

➥ **Close this lesson by praying. Deal ruthlessly with any evidence of pride in your life. Ask the Lord to guide you in specific ways that you can humble yourself.**

As the time for the Lord's Supper draws near, I want us to focus our attention on the Lord and the Supper.

➡ **Which of the following best describes your thoughts as you approach the Lord's Table? Check one or write your own.**

❑ a. Never before have I taken the Lord's Table so seriously. Now that I'm prepared, I am eager to meet my Lord at His Table.

❑ b. God has revealed so much that has been hidden in my heart or that I've tolerated in my life. I tremble at the thought of meeting Him at His Table.

❑ c. God has revealed so many broken relationships in my life, I know I can't get everything reconciled before Supper. I've questioned whether I should come to the Table or not.

❑ d. You've blown this emphasis way out of proportion. Don't expect me to get too serious about the Lord's Table.

❑ e. Other: _____

_____

I pray that our study together has helped you better prepare to partake of the Lord's Table in a worthy manner. Perhaps you may feel overwhelmed by the task of getting your relationships right with God and with others. You may even have thoughts of not attending the service because of the convictions the Holy Spirit has brought to your mind this week. If you are that serious about getting your life right with the Lord, then the Lord's Table probably is just the place for you.

Jesus knows of your weakness and need. He knows your heart. Do you remember what He said to the woman caught in adultery? "'Neither do I condemn you,' Jesus declared. 'Go now and leave your life of sin'" (John 8:11). He doesn't invite you to the Table to condemn you. He is always ready to welcome a *repentant* sinner. If you have put on Christ in salvation, He becomes your "wedding garment." You are welcome at His Table. Remember that Jesus said, "'I have eagerly desired to eat this Passover with you'" (Luke 22:15). He is looking forward to your presence at the Table. Jesus invites you to come.

Are you in need of a fresh cleansing from sin and unrighteousness? Come! Are you weary and burdened? Come! Are you wanting to follow Christ so that you will experience the abundant life He came to give? Come! Are you hungering and thirsting for more in your life and experience of God? Come! The Lord has spiritual food and drink waiting at His Table. The needy are welcomed there. Come to the Lord's Table! He will satisfy your soul.

The following are two meditations from Andrew Murray's *The Lord's Table.* I pray that these thoughts will be a blessing to you as you prepare your mind and heart for the Supper.

In Remembrance of Me

"Do this in remembrance of me" (Luke 22:19, AM). Is this injunction, really necessary? Can it be possible that I should forget Jesus? Forget Jesus? Jesus, who thought of me in eternity; who forgot His own sorrows on the Cross but never forgets mine; who says to me that a mother will sooner forget her nursing child than He in heaven will forget me. Can I forget Jesus? Jesus, my Sun, my Surety, my Bridegroom; my Jesus, without whose love I cannot live. Can I ever forget Jesus?

Ah, me! how often have I forgotten Jesus. How frequently has my foolish heart grieved Him and prepared all kinds of sorrow for itself by forgetting Jesus. At one time it was in the hour of care, or sin, or grief and at another time it was in prosperity and joy that I allowed myself to be led astray. O my soul, be deeply ashamed that You should ever forget Jesus.

And Jesus will not be forgotten. He will see to it that this will not take place for His own sake. He loves us so dearly that He cannot endure to be forgotten. Our love is to Him His happiness and joy. He requires it from us with a holy strictness. So truly has the eternal Love chosen us that it longs to live in our remembrance every day.

For our sakes He will see to it that He is not forgotten. Jesus always yearns to be with us and beside us. He desires that we taste of His crucified love and the power of His heavenly life. Jesus wills that we should always remember Him.

How I long never more to forget Jesus. Thank God, Jesus will so give Himself to me at the table that He will become to me One never to be forgotten. At the table He will overshadow and satisfy me with His love. He will make His love to me so glorious that my love will always hold Him in remembrance. He will unite Himself with me and give His life in me. Out of the power of His own indwelling Spirit in me, it will not be possible for me to forget Him. I have too much considered it a duty and a work to remember Jesus. Lord Jesus, so fill me with Your joy that it will be impossible for me not to remember You.

Jesus remembers me with a tender love. He desires and will grant that the remembrance of Him will always live in me. For this reason He gives me the new remembrance of His love in the Lord's Supper. I will draw near to His table in this joyful assurance: Jesus will there teach me to remember Him always.

Prayer: My Lord, how wonderful is Your love that you always desire to live in my remembrance in my love. Lord, You know that my heart cannot be taught to remember You by force. But as Your love dwells in me, thinking of You becomes a joy—no effort or trouble, but the sweetest rest. Lord, my soul praises You for the wonderful grace of the Supper. First, You give Yourself in Your eternal and unchangeable love as the daily food of my soul. O my Lord, at Your table give Yourself to my soul as its food. Be my food every day, and Your love will keep the thought of You ever living in me. Then I will never forget You; no, not for a single moment. For then I will have no life except in Your love. Amen (*LT*, 74-77).

Forgiveness

"'My blood, which is shed for the forgiveness of sins'" (Matt. 26:28 AM). *Sin*: this word is not to be forgotten at the Lord's Table. It is sin that gives us a right to Christ. It is as a Savior from sin that Christ relates to us. It is as sinners that we sit down at the table. If I cannot always come immediately to Christ and appropriate Him, I can always come on the ground of my sin. Sin is the handle by which I can take hold of Christ. I may not be able to lay my hand on Christ and say: Christ is mine. But I can always say: Sin is mine. Then I hear the glad tidings that Christ died for sin. I obtain courage to say: Sin is mine; and Christ, who died for sin, died also for me. *Sin*: how sweet it is to hear that word from the mouth of Jesus at the table.

And what does my Savior say about sin? He speaks of it only to give the assurance of the forgiveness of sin. That God no more remembers my sin. He no longer counts my sin against me. He does not desire to deal with me in deserved wrath, but He meets me in love as one whose sin is taken away. That is what my Jesus secures for me. He points me to His blood at the table and gives it to me as my own. And that is what you may believe and enjoy, O my soul, when you drink that blood. Ask Him to make known to you the divine glory of this forgiveness as complete, effectual, entire, always valid and eternal. Then you will be able to sing: "Blessed is the man whose transgression is forgiven."

Then will you see how this forgiveness includes in itself all other blessings. For the one of whom God forgives sin, him He also receives, him He loves, him He acknowledges as a child, and gives him the Holy Spirit with all His gifts. The forgiveness of sin is the pledge of entrance into the whole riches of the grace of God. The soul that day by day really enjoys forgiveness in the Lord Jesus will go forth in the joy and power of the Lord.

O what a blessed feast: to know myself to be one with Jesus as a ransomed soul. Blessed it is, because there, while He points with His finger to the sin for which I must be so bitterly ashamed, I can hear this glorious word: "Forgiven." Blessed, because, for the confirmation of this forgiveness and the communication of all its blessing, I am there nourished by the very blood which was shed for forgiveness of sins. Blessed, because in the joy of the forgiveness and the enjoyment of that blood, I am linked again with that Jesus who loves me so wonderfully. Yes, blessed, because I know that in place of sins He now gives me Himself to fill my empty heart, to adorn it with the light and the beauty of His own life. Blessed feast, blessed drinking unto forgiveness of sins!

Prayer: Precious Savior, I am naturally so afraid to look upon my sins, to acknowledge them, and to combat them. In the joy and power of Your forgiveness, I dread this no more. Now I can look upon them as a victor. Help me to love You much, because I have been forgiven much. Amen (*LT*, 85-88).

Pre-Communion Service

If your church has planned a pre-Communion meeting, make every effort to attend. Taking time with the Body of Christ to prepare for the Lord's Table can be a most glorious occasion. As I described briefly for you last week, the preparation meeting of the Moravian Brethren was visited with a deep outpouring of the Holy Spirit's presence. Some were even converted at that time.

➥ **If your church has a pre-Communion service planned, pray now that the Lord will make His presence known in every heart and life. Pray for your brothers and sisters in Christ that each one will be guided to make final preparations for the Lord's Table. Pray for those who may come who do not yet know Christ. Pray that they will come to faith in Christ and be dressed in the "wedding garment" of Christ Himself.**

Fast

Some people find it meaningful to fast leading up to the Lord's Table. You may want to refrain from eating one or more meals (perhaps beginning the evening before the supper) to focus more time in prayer for the service and to heighten your anticipation for the meal.

Week 3

UNTIL HE COMES

*"Whenever you eat this bread and drink this cup,
you proclaim the Lord's death until he comes"*

This week you will conclude your study of *Come to the Lord's Table*. The week begins with your celebration of the Lord's Table. Then because of what Christ did for you on the cross, you will examine ways you can live for Him and express your love for Him. On Day 2 you will be encouraged to take a walk (if you are able) and spend half an hour or more talking to the Lord Jesus in prayer. You can adjust your schedule of lessons to fit this walk into your schedule for the week. Make a special effort to complete these lessons, even if you need extra days next week to complete them all. Because of His sacrifice on the cross, our lives should reflect this truth: "If anyone is in Christ, he is a new creation; the old has gone, the new has come!" (2 Cor. 5:17).

Day 1

CELEBRATE THE LORD'S TABLE

BEFORE SUPPER: ANDREW MURRAY MEDITATIONS

➥ Before going to the Lord's Table today, meditate on what awaits you there. Remember that Jesus Himself eagerly desires this time with you. Realize that He has provided the way for you to come as a worthy guest. Read, reflect, pray, and respond to the Lord through the following meditations from Andrew Murray.

An Exercise of Faith

Prayer: Beloved Lord Jesus, You are the desire of my soul. You are He in whom the love of the Father is disclosed to me. You are He who has loved me even unto death on earth. And You still love me in Your glory on high. You are He in whom alone my soul has its life. Beloved Lord Jesus, my soul cleaves hard to You. On this holy morning I will prepare myself to go to the table by exercising and confessing anew my faith in You....

My Savior, I come to You this morning with the confession that there is nothing in myself on which I can lean. All my experiences confirm to me what You have said of my corruption: that in me, that is, in my flesh, there dwells no good thing. And yet I come to You to lay my claim before You and to take You as mine own. O, my Lord, my claim rests on the word of my Father that He has given His Son for sinners, that You died for the ungodly. My sinfulness is my claim upon You: You are for sinners. My claim is God's eternal righteousness: You have paid the sin-debt; the guilty must go free. My claim rests on Your love: You have compassion on the wretched. My claim is Your faithfulness: O, my Savior, I have given myself to You and You have received me. What You have begun in me, You will gloriously complete.... Blessed Lord, unveil Yourself to me, in order that my faith may be truly strong and joyful.

Yes: Lord Jesus, with all Your fullness You are mine. God be praised, I can say this: Your blood is mine: it has atoned for all my sins. Your righteousness is mine: You, Yourself, are my righteousness, and You make me altogether acceptable to the Father. Your love is mine: yes, in all its height and depth and length and breadth is Your love mine.... All that You have is mine. Your wisdom is mine; Your strength is mine; Your holiness is mine; Your life is mine; Your glory is mine; Your Father is mine. Beloved Lord Jesus, my soul has only one desire this day: that You, my Almighty Friend, would make me with a silent but very powerful activity of faith to behold You, and inwardly appropriate You as my possession. Lord Jesus, in the simplicity of a faith that depends only on You, I say: God be praised, Jesus with all His fullness is mine. How little do I yet thoroughly know or enjoy this truth: Jesus with all His fullness is mine!

Help me now, Lord, to go to Your table in the blessed expectation of new communications out of the treasures of Your love. Let my faith be not only strong, but large: may it cause me to open my mouth wide to receive your holy food.

I stand in need of much today. But what I need above all is this: that I may know my Lord as the daily food of my soul, and that I may comprehend how He will every day be my strength and my life. My desire is that I may understand that not only at the Lord's Supper, but every hour of my life on earth, my Lord Jesus is willing to take the responsibility of my life, to be my life, and to live His life in me.

Beloved Lord, I believe that You have the power to work this in me. I know that Your love is waiting for me, and will take great delight in doing this for me. I believe, Lord, and You will come to help my unbelief. Yes, although I do not thoroughly understand it, I will believe that my Jesus will today communicate Himself anew to me as my life. I will believe that what He does today, He will confirm every day from now on. Yes, my precious Savior, I will this day give myself over to You to dwell in me. And I will believe that You, because You are wholly my possession, will make me ready, come in and take possession of me, and fill me with Yourself. Lord, I do believe; increase this faith within me.

And now, Lord, prepare me and all Your congregation for a blessed observance of the Supper. "Now, unto Him that is able to do exceeding abundantly above all that we ask or think, according to the power that works in us, unto Him be the glory in the Church and in Christ Jesus, unto all generations forever and ever. Amen" (Eph. 3:20-21, AM) (LT, 65-69).

Take, Eat

"Take, eat; this is My body which is given for you" (Matt. 26:26; Luke 22:19, AM). When the Lord says this, He points out to us that His body is not so much His as it is ours. He received it and allowed it to be broken on the cross, not for His own sake, but for ours. He now desires that we should look upon it and take it as our own possession.... The fellowship of the Lord's Supper is a fellowship of giving and taking. Blessed giving: blessed taking.

Blessed giving: the person gives value to the gift. Who is He that gives? It is my Creator, who comes here to give what my soul needs.

It is my Redeemer, who, at the table, will give to me in possession what He has purchased for me.

And what does He give? His body and His blood. He gives the greatest and the best He can bestow. Yes, He gives all that it is possible for Him to give—the broken body which He first offered to the Father as a sacrifice for sin, a sacrifice that filled Him with joy. And what He offered to the Father, to put away sin before Him, He now offers to me, to put away sin in me.

And why does He give this? Because He loves me. He desires to redeem me from death and to bestow on me eternal life in Himself. He gives Himself to me to be the food, the joy, the living power of my soul. O blessed, Heavenly giving of eternal love! Jesus gives me His own body: Jesus gives me Himself.

Blessed taking: it is so simple. Just as I receive with my hand the bread that is intended for me, and hold it before me as my own, so by faith in the word, in which Jesus gives Himself to me, I take Him for myself, and I know that He is really mine. The body in which He suffered for sin is my possession: the power of His atonement is mine. The body of Jesus is my food and my life.

I think of my unworthiness, only to find in it my claim on Him, the Righteous One, who died for the unrighteous. I think of my misery only as the poverty and the hunger for which the meal is prepared, this divine bread so lovingly given. What Jesus in His love would give so heartily and willingly, I will as heartily and freely take.

And so real is the taking. Where God gives, there is power and life. In giving, there is a communication, a real participation of that which is bestowed. Consequently, my taking does not depend on my strength: I have only to receive what my Savior brings to me and inwardly imparts. I, a mere worm, take what He, the Almighty, gives. Blessed giving, blessed taking.

Prayer: Blessed God, may my taking conform with Your giving. What You give, I take as a whole. As You give, so I also receive, — heartily, undividedly, lovingly. Precious Savior, my taking depends wholly on Your giving.

Come and give Yourself truly and with power in the communion of the Spirit. Come, my eternal Redeemer, and let Your love delight itself and be satisfied in me, while You unfold to me the divine secret of the word: "My body given for you." Yes, Lord, I wait upon You. What You give me as my share in Your broken body, that I will take and eat. And my soul will go from Your Table, joyful and strengthened, to thank You and to serve You. Amen. (*LT*, 70-73).

➥ **Now go to the Lord's Table. Worship your wounded Savior. Receive the spiritual food He bestows. Rejoice in Him.**

AFTER SUPPER: WATCH AND PRAY

Now that the Lord's Table has been celebrated, I want you to spend some time in prayer. If you are able, I want you to work through the remainder of this lesson with some fellow Christians—perhaps you will do this immediately following the Lord's Table. If not then, try to arrange a time to join with other Christians for as much as one hour. I suggest that you choose other believers of the same sex for this prayer time.

➡ **Check one of the following ways you will complete this lesson.**

❏ a. I will pray with a small group of no more than eight.

❏ b. I will pray in a "triplet"—me and two others.

❏ c. I will pray by myself.

Over the past week or two, God has been working with you to put away sin. You may have become painfully aware of areas of your own weaknesses—temptations to sin where you are weak to resist. I pray that you now have entered a new resolve to live a life that is worthy of the sacrifice Jesus paid for you on the cross.

➡ **Read the following hymn. What does the writer say we owe Jesus? Underline it.**

Jesus Paid It All
Elvina M. Hall

I hear the Saviour say, "Thy strength indeed is small,
    Child of weakness, watch and pray, Find in Me thine all in all."

Lord, now indeed I find Thy pow'r, and Thine alone,
    Can change the leper's spots And melt the heart of stone.

For nothing good have I Whereby Thy grace to claim;
    I'll wash my garments white In the blood of Calv'ry's Lamb.

And when, before the throne, I stand in Him complete,
    "Jesus died my soul to save," My lips shall still repeat.

Refrain
Jesus paid it all, All to Him I owe;
    Sin had left a crimson stain, He wash'd it white as snow.

Jesus gave His all for us. We owe our all to Him. Paul said it this way, "I urge you to live a life worthy of the calling you have received" (Eph. 4:1). We cannot be strong enough in ourselves to live such a life. We need Him. You need to be strong in the face of temptation. Jesus has a way for you to be strong against temptation. Following the Last Supper, Jesus spoke a warning to Peter.

➥ **As you read this Scripture, underline the warning(s).**

"Simon, Simon, Satan has asked to sift you as wheat. But I have prayed for you, Simon, that your faith may not fail. And when you have turned back, strengthen your brothers."

But he replied, "Lord, I am ready to go with you to prison and to death."

Jesus answered, "I tell you, Peter, before the rooster crows today, you will deny three times that you know me" (Luke 22:31-34).

Jesus warned Peter that his faith was about to be tested by Satan. When Peter affirmed his willingness to die with Jesus, Jesus explained that he would wind up denying Him that very night. Then Jesus took His disciples across the valley and up on the Mount of Olives to the Garden of Gethsemane. To eight of the disciples, Jesus said, "Sit here while I go over there and pray" (Matt. 26:36).

➥ **Underline what Jesus asked Peter, James, and John (a "triplet") to do while He prayed—the first time and again after he found them asleep. Answer the questions that follow.**

He took Peter and the two sons of Zebedee along with him, and he began to be sorrowful and troubled. Then he said to them, "My soul is overwhelmed with sorrow to the point of death. Stay here and keep watch with me."

Going a little farther, he fell with his face to the ground and prayed, "My Father, if it is possible, may this cup be taken from me. Yet not as I will, but as you will."

Then he returned to his disciples and found them sleeping. "Could you men not keep watch with me for one hour?" he asked Peter. "Watch and pray so that you will not fall into temptation. The spirit is willing, but the body is weak" (Matt. 26:36-41).

➥ **Q1. Why did Jesus ask them to watch and pray?**
so they would not... _____

Q2. Why did they fall asleep? because the body was _____

Jesus asked them to watch with Him and then to watch and pray so they would not fall into temptation. Instead of praying, they yielded to the weakness of their bodies and slept. Jesus addressed this second message to Peter. He knew that Peter would not be prepared for the time of testing he was about to face because he had not spent time in prayer. Because Peter allowed his body (flesh) to win out over his Spirit, Peter failed in his time of testing and denied the Lord. Later he went out and wept bitterly because of his sin. This is an example of why wo muot bo pooplo of prayor. Prayor io whoro wo goin God's strength through the Holy Spirit to resist temptation to sin.

What a Friend We Have in Jesus
Joseph Scriven

What a friend we have in Jesus, All our sins and griefs to bear!
  What a privilege to carry Ev'rything to God in prayer!
Oh, what peace we often forfeit, Oh, what needless pain we bear,
  All because we do not carry Ev'rything to God in prayer!

Have we trials and temptations? Is there trouble anywhere?
  We should never be discouraged, Take it to the Lord in prayer:
Can we find a friend so faithful Who will all our sorrows share?
  Jesus knows our ev'ry weakness, Take it to the Lord in prayer.

Are we weak and heavy laden, Cumbered with a load of care?
  Precious Saviour, still our refuge; Take it to the Lord in prayer:
Do thy friends despise, forsake thee? Take it to the Lord in prayer;
  In His arms He'll take and shield thee; Thou wilt find a solace there.

➥ **Pray together (or alone if you must). Continue praying as long as time permits, or until you sense you have achieved God's desires for this prayer time.**

- Take some time thanking Jesus for His sacrifice for your sins.
- Confess to Him your desire to live worthy lives as well as your dependence on Him for help to do so.
- "Confess [your] faults one to another, and pray one for another, that ye may be healed" (James 5:16, KJV). Share general areas of past weaknesses or sin or present areas of temptation (e.g. honesty, clean language, pure thought-life, moral purity, forgiveness, obedience, faithful stewardship, etc.). Pray for each other regarding specific areas of need. You might ask each other, "How may we pray for your spiritual victory over sin?" If you are praying alone, talk to Jesus about these matters. Jesus lives to intercede for you! (Heb. 7:25).
- Pray for your church and her leadership (both paid and volunteer) that they will be pure, holy, Godly, and victorious over sin.
- Pray for specific church members, groups, or families that they will be strong and victorious over sin.

When Jesus died, He paid the penalty for our sin and made for-giveness available to us. We all need that forgiveness. Some need to know His healing touch as well. In today's lesson I want to address a spiritual healing that some of you may need. The assignment may be something you will complete later when you have ample time. That is okay. Some of you will not identify with the needs described in this lesson and that also is okay.

I've found that some Christians are not experiencing the full dimensions of a love relationship with God. They want to love God and be loved by Him, but they consciously or unconsciously keep Him at a distance. They can never seem to experience a closeness to God as heavenly Father. Sometimes they get very involved in church related activities seeking an experience of God's love that seems elusive.

➡ **How would you describe your own experience of an inti-mate love relationship with your heavenly Father? Check one or write your own.**

❑ a. I've experienced a very close, personal, loving relationship with Him.

❑ b. I've felt a longing for that love and closeness, but I can't ever seem to experience what I know should be true of that relationship with Him.

❑ c. For some reason, I have a fear of God and I just will not allow Him to get close to me. It's like I say, "God, I want you to love me, just don't come too close."

❑ d. My knowledge of God's love has been almost exclusively a head knowledge. I've never sought a personal relationship.

❑ e. Other: _____

_____

If you checked a, you may want to skip to "A Walk to Emmaus" on page 91. If you have not experienced a closeness to your heavenly Father, the problem could be sin in your own life. If that is the case you need to repent and return to Him. Last week's lessons were designed to help you do that. I've encountered a variety of other reasons for this sense of distance from God. Those reasons have included:

- One or both parents were abusive (verbally, physically, or sexually).
- A parent (especially when it was a father) was not present to show love because of death, abandonment, divorce, or physical disability.
- One or both parents neglected a child because of work commitments, drug or alcohol abuse, or emotional problems of their own.
- A spiritual leader or a significant other person was abusive emotionally, physically, or sexually.
- And the list could go on...

In these cases your problem may stem from the sin of others, not your own sin. Or it may not be anyone's sin, but some unfortunate circumstances. Now, if you respond to these circumstances by sinning yourself, you need to deal with your sin. We dealt with that last week in the lesson on "Reconcile and Forgive." But you may have a wounded spirit that needs to be healed. Not only do you need to experience Jesus' forgiveness, you need to experience His healing touch as well. Perhaps you are spiritually needy like the woman in the following Scripture was physically needy:

> Just then a woman who had been subject to bleeding for twelve years came up behind him and touched the edge of his cloak. She said to herself, "If I only touch his cloak, I will be healed."
>
> Jesus turned and saw her. "Take heart, daughter," he said, "your faith has healed you." And the woman was healed from that moment (Matt. 9:20-22).

➡ **Do you sense a need for some sort of spiritual healing that you know only Jesus can give?** ❑ Yes ❑ No

➡ **If so, even if you cannot explain or identify the reason for your need, ask the Lord to act as your Great Physician and do the healing work He knows you need. Check here if you prayed and asked for His healing touch.** ❑

I spoke to a woman who had been abused as a child. She was one who kept God at a distance because of her fears. She needed to know God's safe, pure, gentle, trustworthy love. She knew about His love in her head. But what she needed was to *experience* His love so she would know it in her heart. God had permitted her to be overwhelmed with problems. That was an ideal time for her to experience God's love.

We prayed and I recommended that she get alone with her heavenly Father, drop her guard, and allow Him to love her. I didn't know how He might do that, but I knew that He was the only One who could reveal His love in the way she needed it. I couldn't explain His love any more than she already knew intellectually.

She came back the next day to tell me her story. She spent the afternoon in a garden alone with her heavenly Father. Somehow He revealed His love to her in a way she was overwhelmed by the peace and comfort she found there. Months later she told me it was like God had given her a heart transplant.

On another occasion I spoke with a woman whose father had been a workaholic. He never seemed to have time for his daughter. She was having difficulty feeling a closeness to her heavenly Father when she went to worship. As we talked, she described her regular desire to pray. When I prayed with her, I asked the Lord something I had never prayed before. I said, "Lord, Your Word says that because of sin, no one seeks after You. Since my sister is sensing a desire to pray that must be your invitation for her to spend time with you. Would you help her to interpret her every desire to pray as your invitation for a Father-daughter date?"

After the prayer, I explained that her heavenly Father loved her dearly and He wanted to spend time with His daughter; He wanted to reveal His love to her. Months later I received a letter from her. She said, "I've had many Father-daughter dates since we talked. It's been wonderful! And now when I go to worship, I feel a deep love for God because I have experienced His love for me."

If you are having difficulty experiencing a closeness to your heavenly Father, you need to understand that He wants to reveal His love to you more than you want to experience it. You need to let Him.

➡ **I want to suggest that you go on a Father-daughter date (for girls/women) or a Father-son outing (for boys/men). Spend this time with your heavenly Father as soon as you can set aside the time. Try to do it in the next week or two while the experience of the Lord's Table is fresh on your mind.**

- Go to a favorite spot or a quiet place where you can be alone with your Father (perhaps an outdoor place). Allow for an extended period of time—an hour or maybe several hours.

- Don't worry about what to say. God's love is unconditional. Your experience of His love is not dependent on your praying the right prayer, claiming the right promise, or quoting the right Scripture. Just get alone with Him, and let Him love you.
- If you've been wounded in your past, tell your Father all about the pain. Let Him lance the wound in your spirit and drain out all the corruption. Ask Him to heal the wound and take away the pain. Because:
  "There is a balm in Gilead to make the wounded whole;
  There is a balm in Gilead to heal the sin-sick soul."
- Ask Him to forgive you and cleanse you for any bitterness and unforgiveness or sin on your own part. Ask Him for help to forgive anyone who has offended you. Jesus can help you here.
- Give Him permission to reveal His love to you in any way He chooses. Become like a little child again. Allow your heavenly Father to wrap His loving arms around you and hold you close. Receive His love.
- Every time you feel a desire to pray or a desire to spend time with Him, interpret that as His invitation for time with you— His child. Give Him all the time He wants. He will fill up the emptiness or void in your life. His love is sufficient.
- Understand, too, that this may be a process for you over a period of time and not just an event where God breaks through. Let God do the work on His time table. He loves you; He will not leave you like an orphan.

➥ **Keep a brief journal of your times alone with your heavenly Father. Record ways He reveals His love to you, things you have talked (prayed) about, feelings of comfort and healing, and so forth. Use extra paper as needed.**

_____

_____

_____

_____

_____

_____

_____

_____

_____

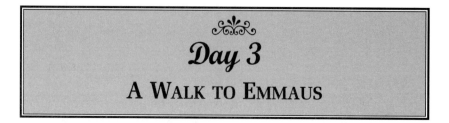

Day 3
A Walk to Emmaus

➡ **Take a moment to remember the crucifixion Jesus endured for you and me at Calvary.**

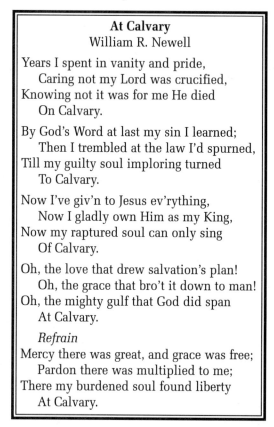

At Calvary
William R. Newell

Years I spent in vanity and pride,
   Caring not my Lord was crucified,
Knowing not it was for me He died
   On Calvary.

By God's Word at last my sin I learned;
   Then I trembled at the law I'd spurned,
Till my guilty soul imploring turned
   To Calvary.

Now I've giv'n to Jesus ev'rything,
   Now I gladly own Him as my King,
Now my raptured soul can only sing
   Of Calvary.

Oh, the love that drew salvation's plan!
   Oh, the grace that bro't it down to man!
Oh, the mighty gulf that God did span
   At Calvary.

Refrain
Mercy there was great, and grace was free;
   Pardon there was multiplied to me;
There my burdened soul found liberty
   At Calvary.

On Sunday afternoon, the day of Jesus' resurrection, two men took an unexpected walk with the Lord. As you read their story, see if you can imagine what it must have been like to have Jesus as your personal teacher along the way.

> Now that same day two of them were going to a village called Emmaus, about seven miles from Jerusalem. They were talking with each other about everything that had hap-

pened. As they talked and discussed these things with each other, Jesus himself came up and walked along with them; but they were kept from recognizing him.

He asked them, "What are you discussing together as you walk along?"

They stood still, their faces downcast. One of them, named Cleopas, asked him, "Are you only a visitor to Jerusalem and do not know the things that have happened there in these days?"

"What things?" he asked.

"About Jesus of Nazareth," they replied. "He was a prophet, powerful in word and deed before God and all the people. The chief priests and our rulers handed him over to be sentenced to death, and they crucified him; but we had hoped that he was the one who was going to redeem Israel. And what is more, it is the third day since all this took place. In addition, some of our women amazed us. They went to the tomb early this morning but didn't find his body. They came and told us that they had seen a vision of angels, who said he was alive. Then some of our companions went to the tomb and found it just as the women had said, but him they did not see."

He said to them, "How foolish you are, and how slow of heart to believe all that the prophets have spoken! Did not the Christ have to suffer these things and then enter his glory?" And beginning with Moses and all the Prophets, he explained to them what was said in all the Scriptures concerning himself.

As they approached the village to which they were going, Jesus acted as if he were going farther. But they urged him strongly, "Stay with us, for it is nearly evening; the day is almost over." So he went in to stay with them.

When he was at the table with them, he took bread, gave thanks, broke it and began to give it to them. Then their eyes were opened and they recognized him, and he disappeared from their sight. They asked each other, "Were not our hearts burning within us while he talked with us on the road and opened the Scriptures to us?"

They got up and returned at once to Jerusalem. There they found the Eleven and those with them, assembled together and saying, "It is true! The Lord has risen and has appeared to Simon." Then the two told what had happened on the way, and how Jesus was recognized by them when he broke the bread (Luke 24:13-35).

➡ I want you to take a walk and talk with your Lord (or find a quiet place to sit and talk with Him). Too often our prayer times are hurried or filled with requests. Try to get away from your busy world and spend half an hour or more with Jesus—with no set agenda. Just spend time talking with Him as a friend who has given His life for you. Enjoy His presence. Before you go, read or sing "In the Garden" and then go alone with Him to your special place.

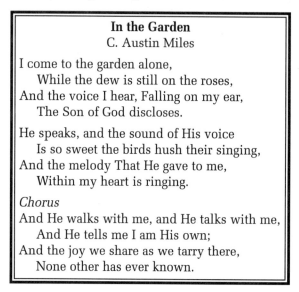

In the Garden
C. Austin Miles

I come to the garden alone,
  While the dew is still on the roses,
And the voice I hear, Falling on my ear,
  The Son of God discloses.

He speaks, and the sound of His voice
  Is so sweet the birds hush their singing,
And the melody That He gave to me,
  Within my heart is ringing.

Chorus
And He walks with me, and He talks with me,
  And He tells me I am His own;
And the joy we share as we tarry there,
  None other has ever known.

AFTER YOUR WALK

➡ Reflect on your walk/talk with Jesus. On the lines below, summarize your thoughts or feelings following your time alone with Jesus.

_____

_____

_____

_____

_____

_____

_____

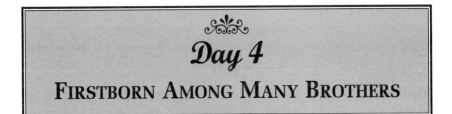

Day 4

FIRSTBORN AMONG MANY BROTHERS

After the Last Supper, Jesus went to Gethsemane to pray. He then was taken captive, put on trial, and crucified the next day. He was buried in a borrowed tomb, and on Sunday morning He arose from the grave—a victor over sin and death! Colossians 1:18 describes Him as "the beginning and the *firstborn* from among the dead."

Jesus is described by Paul in Romans 8:29 as "the *firstborn among many brothers*." He is our holy Elder Brother since we have been adopted into God's family as sons and daughters of God.

➨ **Read Romans 8:28-29 below and underline what God predestined us to be.**

"We know that in all things God works for the good of those who love him, who have been called according to his purpose. For those God foreknew he also predestined to be conformed to the likeness of his Son, that he might be the firstborn among many brothers" (Rom. 8:28-29).

God predestined us "to be conformed to the likeness of his Son." God's determined purpose is that we become like Christ. He uses all the experiences of life—both the good and the bad—to chip away all the things in us that do not look like Christ so that what remains is like Christ.

I once heard a story told about a sculptor (I think it was Michelangelo). Someone asked him how he could carve such a beautiful angel out of the lump of marble. He said, "There is an angel in there. I just chip away everything that is not angel." When you came to faith in Christ, God placed the Holy Spirit of Christ in you. Now He is at working chipping away everything that doesn't look like Christ so that you will be like Him.

➨ **Read the following Scriptures and underline the words or phrases that describe how we will be like Christ. I've underlined the first one for you.**

1 John 4:17—In this way, love is made complete among us so that we will have confidence on the day of judgment, because in this world <u>we are like him</u>.

Colossians 3:10—[We] have put on the new self, which is being renewed in knowledge in the image of its Creator.

1 Corinthians 2:16—We have the mind of Christ.

1 Corinthians 15:49—Just as we have borne the likeness of the earthly man, so shall we bear the likeness of the man from heaven.

2 Corinthians 3:18—We, who with unveiled faces all reflect the Lord's glory, are being transformed into his likeness with ever-increasing glory, which comes from the Lord, who is the Spirit.

1 John 3:2-3—Dear friends, now we are children of God, and what we will be has not yet been made known. But we know that when he appears, we shall be like him, for we shall see him as he is. Everyone who has this hope in him purifies himself, just as he is pure.

➡ **Based on these Scriptures, which of the following will be true about those who are God's children? Check one.**
❑ a. We will never be like Christ. Our nature is too sinful.
❑ b. God is working to make us like Christ. In eternity we will be like Him.

➡ **Based upon that last Scripture (1 John 3:2-3), since we have the hope of being like Christ what will we do to ourselves? Fill in the blanks:** "Everyone who has this hope in him... _____ himself, just as he is _____."

➡ **Since God is working to make you like Christ, what still remains in you that mars (distorts, blemishes, or hides) the image of Christ in you? Check any or all that apply.**
❑ pride/arrogance instead of humility
❑ disobedience instead of perfect obedience
❑ love for the world and things of the world rather than love for God with all my being (heart, soul, mind, and strength)
❑ lust for influence, power rather than a willingness to be a lowly servant of all
❑ selfish ambition rather than seeking first His Kingdom
❑ lack of submission to His lordship
❑ prayerlessness
❑ lust of the flesh—food, pleasure, sex, etc.
❑ lust of the eyes

- ❑ apathy
- ❑ lack of love, compassion
- ❑ harshness instead of gentleness
- ❑ wanting to rule rather than serve
- ❑ selfishness
- ❑ unforgiveness
- ❑ strife or conflict with others
- ❑ lack of submission to Christ, rebellion
- ❑ uncontrolled tongue, gossip, slander
- ❑ dishonesty/untruthfulness
- ❑ unmerciful
- ❑ prejudice
- ❑ Others? _____

None of us will be fully like Christ this side of heaven. But some Christians have the faulty view that they must continuously live in sin. I've heard Christians say, "I sin every day" as if it were a necessity. We can grow in Christlikeness because the Holy Spirit of Christ lives in us to enable our victory over sin.

➡ **Read the following verses from Romans 6 and underline the words or phrases that describe our new relationship to sin because we have died to our old sinful nature and have been raised to walk a new life in Christ. I've underlined one for you.**

What shall we say, then? Shall we go on sinning so that grace may increase? By no means! We died to sin; how can we live in it any longer?...

Our old self was crucified with him so that the body of sin might be done away with, that we should no longer be slaves to sin—because anyone who has died has been freed from sin....

Sin shall not be your master, because you are not under law, but under grace.

What then? Shall we sin because we are not under law but under grace? By no means!... You have been set free from sin and have become slaves to righteousness....

But now that you have been set free from sin and have become slaves to God, the benefit you reap leads to holiness, and the result is eternal life. (Rom. 6:1-2, 6-7, 14, 15, 18, 22).

We are dead to sin. Sin no longer is our master; we've been set free from sin. With the power of the indwelling Holy Spirit we can live as slaves of God and slaves to righteousness. Though you may fail to live in this victory, it is possible to live increasingly victorious over sin. Brothers and sisters in Christ, let's start living up to our birthright!

God will continue His work of molding and shaping us more and more into the likeness of His Son. We can cooperate with Him or resist Him. We can cooperate with Him by studying the life of Christ and allowing the Holy Spirit to conform us to His likeness. We also cooperate with Him by repenting of sin when He reveals it, and returning to the Lord and His ways. Two things can prompt our repentance.

➥ **Underline in these Scriptures things that lead to repentance.**

Godly sorrow brings repentance that leads to salvation and leaves no regret, but worldly sorrow brings death (2 Cor. 7:10).

Do you show contempt for the riches of his kindness, tolerance and patience, not realizing that God's kindness leads you toward repentance? (Rom. 2:4).

Godly sorrow can bring about repentance. This is a grief over sin that leads to turning away from sin to God. Recognizing the body of Christ and it is as if you drive the nail, you spit on Him, you use the whip every time you sin—this can produce this grief and godly sorrow that leads you to repent. God's kindness can also lead you to repentance. God's character of love, mercy, and gentleness can lead you to love and obey Him in response to His undeserved kindness. I pray that this study and the celebration of the Lord's Table has increased both your sense of godly sorrow for your sin and your sense of God's unbelievable kindness demonstrated at the cross.

➥ **Do you desire to be like Jesus? Do you yearn to live, act, and speak in a way that will reflect Jesus to the world around you?** ❑ Yes ❑ No

➥ **If you answered "yes," write a prayer to Jesus telling Him so.**

_____

_____

_____

_____

_____

_____

➥ **Read the text of the song "Whatever It Takes" on the next page. As you read, underline words or phrases that describe what the songwriter is willing to do to draw closer and be more like Christ our Lord. I've underlined one for you.**

There's a voice calling me from an old rugged tree,
    And it whispers, "Draw closer to Me;
Leave this world far behind, there are new heights to climb,
    And a new place in Me you will find."

Chorus
For whatever it takes to draw closer to You, Lord,
    That's what I'll be willing to do;
For whatever it takes to be more like You,
    That's what I'll be willing to do.

Take the dearest things to me, if that's how it must be
    To draw me closer to You;
Let the disappointments come, lonely days without the sun,
    If through sorrow more like You I'll become.

Take my houses and lands, change my dreams and my plans,
    For I'm placing my whole life in Your hands;
And if you call me today to a land far away,
    Lord, I'll go and Your will obey.

Chorus
I'll trade sunshine for rain, comfort for pain,
    That's what I'll be willing to do;
For whatever it takes for my will to break,
    That's what I'll be willing to do.

➥ **In view of His death for you on the cross, check items below you believe you would be willing to do to draw closer to Him.**
  ❑ He can take (at His request I'll give) the dearest things to me.
  ❑ I'll accept disappointments, sorrow, and sunless days.
  ❑ He can have my houses and lands if that's what He wants.
  ❑ He can change my dreams and my plans.
  ❑ I'll place my whole life in His hands.
  ❑ He can call me to go on mission with Him to a faraway land.
  ❑ I'll trade sunshine for rain.
  ❑ I'll trade comfort for pain.
  ❑ I'll do WHATEVER it takes to be more like Him...

➥ **Conclude today's lesson in prayer. Express to the Lord your desire to become more like Him. Give Him permission to work in your life to accomplish His perfect work in you.**

Day 5

LOVE ONE ANOTHER

God so loved you and me that He gave His only Son to pay a death penalty for our sin. He loved us and met our need for a Savior. At the Last Supper with His disciples, Jesus gave us a new commandment:

> "A new command I give you: Love one another. As I have loved you, so you must love one another. By this all men will know that you are my disciples, if you love one another" (John 13:34-35).

Jesus gave us the example of love. Now as we reflect that same love to our fellow Christians the world will recognize that we are disciples (followers) of Jesus Christ. Love is a choice you make to seek the best for another person. How do you go about showing love to one another? The Apostle John gives us some answers.

➡ **Read the following two Scriptures and underline ways we can show love to our brothers (and sisters) in Christ.**

> If anyone has material possessions and sees his brother in need but has no pity on him, how can the love of God be in him? Dear children, let us not love with words or tongue but with actions and in truth (1 John 3:17-18).

> This is how we know what love is: Jesus Christ laid down his life for us. And we ought to lay down our lives for our brothers (1 John 3:16).

We show love by meeting needs. Love is not a feeling or words, it is an action that meets a need. We also can show love by laying down our lives for our brothers. Most of us will read that verse and assume that it doesn't apply to us because we are not likely to be asked to lay down our physical lives. Don't pass over it too quickly.

I was leading revival services in a church that was deeply divided over a number of issues. One issue was the style of music worship used in the Sunday services. Some wanted to return to the traditional use of a hymnal led by a music leader. Others enjoyed the use of praise choruses displayed by an overhead projector and led by a praise team. I spoke on loving one another enough to lay down yourself in love for your brothers and sisters in Christ. I didn't suggest any specifics, but I did suggest that we can lay down our personal opinions, preferences, desires, plans, dreams, and things out of love for others.

The next night the leader of the praise team came to me. She said God convicted her in the service the night before that the praise team needed to lay down their music leadership out of love for the rest of the body. When she called the other team members, God had said the same thing to them as well. That night they all came at the invitation time and publicly resigned and asked forgiveness for causing division in the body. They said, "We love you too much to continue being a source of division. We are laying down the praise team because we love you." That is love in action, not just in words.

Divisions in a church over worship style indicate that worship is tending toward ritual rather than genuine encounter with the living God. In this case the issue was not whether one style of music leadership was better than the other—as far as the Lord is concerned either would be acceptable if the hearts are right. The issue was that people were holding on to their own personal preferences and dividing the Body of Christ rather than showing love. Either side could have laid down their preferences out of love for the body and God would have been pleased. Unity and love are important to God.

➤ **Ask God if there is anything He would ask you to lay down out of love for your brothers and sisters in Christ. If there is an area of division between you and other believers, ask the Lord how you can show your love in actions rather than just in words. If you know of a believer who has a need, ask God what, if anything, He would have you lay down to meet that need. Does He want you to lay down or give away any of the following? Check any that God speaks to you about.**

❑ a material possession	❑ money
❑ my preferences	❑ my opinion
❑ my dream or goal	❑ my desires
❑ an attitude	❑ a behavior
❑ a schedule	❑ an activity
❑ a position of leadership	❑ time to serve others
❑ resistance to change	❑ my comfort or security
❑ opposition to a project	❑ my expectations
❑ withholding of support	❑ my rights
❑ my reputation	❑ my life, if God asks for it

➤ **Pray that God will help your church truly love one another.**

Day 6

FORGIVENESS AND LOVE

Jesus went to the house of a Pharisee for a meal. While they were eating, a woman "who had lived a sinful life in that town" (Luke 7:37) anointed Jesus' feet with perfume and wiped them with her hair. Simon the Pharisee thought Jesus should have rejected her because of her sinful past. Jesus told him a parable:

> "Two men owed money to a certain moneylender. One owed him five hundred denarii, and the other fifty. Neither of them had the money to pay him back, so he canceled the debts of both. Now which of them will love him more?"
>
> Simon replied, "I suppose the one who had the bigger debt canceled."
>
> "You have judged correctly," Jesus said....
>
> "Do you see this woman? I came into your house. You did not give me any water for my feet, but she wet my feet with her tears and wiped them with her hair. You did not give me a kiss, but this woman, from the time I entered, has not stopped kissing my feet. You did not put oil on my head, but she has poured perfume on my feet. Therefore, I tell you, her many sins have been forgiven—for she loved much. But he who has been forgiven little loves little" (Luke 7:41-47).

➥ **Think about your own life of sin, rebellion against God, neglect of Him, or your repeated offenses that He has forgiven. Which of the following best describes your love? Check one.**
❑ a. I've been forgiven so much, I can't help but love Him deeply.
❑ b. I don't think He's had to forgive me very much, and my love for Him is shallow.
❑ c. Just knowing that He gave His life for me causes me to love Him much.
❑ d. For some reason I do not feel much love toward Christ.

We are the recipients of the love of God that He demonstrated to us through Christ and His death on the cross. What a great love! We've been forgiven. Our sin debt has been paid. If your love for

Him is small, I pray that God will open your eyes to see the greatness of the love He has lavished on you and that God will enable you to know that love experientially. If you love Him much, you will want to express that love. But Jesus is in heaven. How can you express your love for Him? Jesus described Judgment Day when the King will commend His "sheep:"

"'I was hungry and you gave me something to eat, I was thirsty and you gave me something to drink, I was a stranger and you invited me in, I needed clothes and you clothed me, I was sick and you looked after me, I was in prison and you came to visit me.'

"Then the righteous will answer him, 'Lord, when did we see you hungry and feed you, or thirsty and give you something to drink? When did we see you a stranger and invite you in, or needing clothes and clothe you? When did we see you sick or in prison and go to visit you?'

"The King will reply, 'I tell you the truth, whatever you did for one of the least of these brothers of mine, you did for me.'" (Matthew 25:34-40)

One way you can express your love for Jesus is by loving others. Watch for ways you can show love for others by meeting their needs.

Yesterday, you examined the new command of Jesus to love one another. Is your church planning a love feast at the conclusion of this study? If so, you may have been asked to consider giving a special thank or love offering. This will be an opportunity for you to give an extra special offering to say, "Thank you, Jesus, for giving your life for me!" We can never repay Him, but we can express our love by loving those for whom He died. This offering should be freely given or not given at all. It should be in addition to your regular tithe or giving to God's work. If God identified a heart idol that is of value that you need to give away, that may be the thing to give (or sell and give the proceeds) for your love offering.

➡ **If your church is planning to receive a love offering, prayerfully think about what you would like to give to express your love to Christ and the Body of Christ. If your church is not receiving an offering, you may want to think of another way to express your love to Christ and "one another" through a special gift. What, if anything, have you decided to give?**

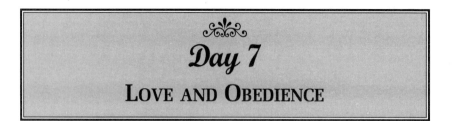

Day 7
LOVE AND OBEDIENCE

We've reached the end of our study together. I pray that God has rekindled in you a first love for Christ. He longs to draw you closer and closer to Himself. If you still find that your love for the Lord is not what you know it should be, continue to seek the Lord.

• Spend time with your Lord. Take some more walks with Him.
• Ask Him to reveal His love to you in a way that you will know His love by experience.
• Spend time reviewing the lessons in week 1 to know His sacrificial love for you on the cross.
• Review the lessons in week 2 and seek to get right in your relationship with the Lord.
• And finally, begin to obey Him.

Obedience is directly connected to love for the Lord.

➡ **Read the following Scriptures and circle the words *love (loves, loved)* and *obey(s)* each time they occur.**

John 14:15—"If you love me, you will obey what I command."

John 14:21—"Whoever has my commands and obeys them, he is the one who loves me. He who loves me will be loved by my Father, and I too will love him and show myself to him."

John 14:23-24—"If anyone loves me, he will obey my teaching. My Father will love him, and we will come to him and make our home with him. He who does not love me will not obey my teaching."

➡ **Q1. What will the one who loves Jesus do with His commands?**

_____

Q2. If you love and obey Him, how will Jesus and the Father respond to you?

(v. 21) _____

(vv. 23-24) _____

When you love Jesus, you will obey what He commands. When you love and obey Him, He and the Father will love you in an added dimension. Jesus will reveal Himself to you and They will take up residence in your life in a new way. Obedience is one of the characteristics of Jesus Himself. He said, "My food... is to do the will of him who sent me and to finish his work" (John 4.34). Paul said, "he humbled himself and became obedient to death—even death on a cross! (Phil. 2:8). When you love Jesus and seek to live like Him you will obey Him.

The Final Command

After Jesus' resurrection, He spent 40 days instructing His disciples. On several occasions He commanded them to carry the good news of salvation to all the peoples of the earth. He wanted to make sure that they did not miss this final command, because all His ministry and sacrifice would be wasted if they failed to obey Him.

➡ **Read and underline the final command below.**

> "Go and make disciples of all nations, baptizing them in the name of the Father and of the Son and of the Holy Spirit, and teaching them to obey everything I have commanded you" (Matt. 28:19-20).

Just before Jesus ascended into heaven, He reminded His disciples one more time: "you will receive power when the Holy Spirit comes on you; and you will be my witnesses in Jerusalem, and in all Judea and Samaria, and to the ends of the earth" (Acts 1:8). Why should we (as His present day disciples) obey this final command? Paul wrote to the Corinthian church about the ministry God has assigned to us to reconcile men to God.

➡ **Read 2 Corinthians 5:14-15 below and underline the reason we should give ourselves for others to know Christ.**

> Christ's love compels us, because we are convinced that one died for all, and therefore all died. And he died for all, that those who live should no longer live for themselves but for him who died for them and was raised again (2 Cor. 5:14-15).

➡ **Out of love for your Lord, will you pray and surrender yourself to obey the final command?**_____

If you will, God will help you know what your part is. Work together with your church to reap the harvest that Christ says is already ripe. If you would like help, I have prepared a book like this one to help you and your church obey the final command (see page 108). Out of love for Christ let's adopt the battle cry of Moravian missions:

"To win for the Lamb that was slain the reward of His sufferings."

Pastor's Guide

[Note: Read the preface (pp. 7-8) if you have not yet done so.]

Dear Pastor, you are probably reading this page in this book because you realize the importance of giving greater emphasis to proper preparation for the Lord's Table (or Lord's Supper, Communion, or the Eucharist). I have attempted to put together a resource that can help your people focus on the sacrifice of Jesus on the cross and return to their first love for Christ. I guide them through a fairly thorough self-examination to help them get right with God and others before the Holy Supper. I want them to be prepared to partake in a worthy manner. Then I challenge them to live a more godly life of obedience and service to Christ because of His sacrifice for them. I pray that this tool will assist you in helping your people experience genuine renewal of life and vitality for Christ.

You may come up with a wide variety of ways you could use *Come to the Lord's Table*, but let me briefly summarize a possible use plan for this resource.

Overview of the Process

1. **Invitation.** Invite all your members to prepare for and attend a sacred assembly of the church around a Lord's Table observance. Use the calendar on page 112 to schedule your events. If you choose to expand the study to four weeks to allow more time to respond to the lessons, use the calendar on page 111.

2. **Personal Preparations.** Distribute copies of *Come to the Lord's Table* to each adult and older youth member. Allow for at least three weeks of preparation prior to the date of the Lord's Table. Ask each member to complete the daily assignments for three weeks before the Supper.

3. **Pre-Communion Service.** (Recommended) On the day before the Lord's Table conduct a pre-Communion service (described below) as a time for final preparations for individual members and your church body as a whole.

4. **Celebrate the Lord's Table.** Spend your entire service with a focus on the Holy Supper and the sacrifice of Jesus on the cross that it represents. Build your message and worship around the theme of the supper and the cross.

5. **Challenge to Godly Living.** Following the week of the Supper, encourage members to use the daily lessons in Week 3 to choose to live a godly life for Christ.
6. **Love Feast.** (Optional) Some time following the final week of lessons, conduct a "love feast" (described below) to feast, worship, and share testimonies of God's work in your lives.

Using *Come to the Lord's Table*

Pray. Your church belongs to the Lord Jesus who is her Head. Begin this process with prayer. Ask the Lord to guide you to Himself. Invite prayer warriors and prayer ministry teams to bathe this season in prayer. Pray for specific members, every member, that this will be a time of renewal and revival for every life and family. Pray that lost people will even be converted during this season.

Decide on the Season for the Emphasis. You can use this guide any time of year. The season leading up to Easter may be an especially meaningful time, since it coincides with the Last Supper Jesus celebrated with His disciples before going to the cross. Some churches may schedule a special Maundy Thursday service during Easter week to commemorate the Last Supper. Others may choose to use it in the winter leading up to a special Christmas observance of the Lord's Table with a love feast on New Year's Eve. Others will choose a time around Thanksgiving. Sometimes "now" is the most appropriate time. Use it leading up to your next scheduled Lord's Table. You might even use it as spiritual preparation for revival or evangelistic meetings.

Determine the Schedule. Read through this section of suggestions and decide whether you will conduct a pre-Communion service and the love feast in conjunction with the Lord's Table observance. Set the dates on your church calendar. If possible, clear the three weeks for this emphasis of competing events or church activities so people will not be distracted from their preparations.

Order Books. You can order bulk quantities of *Come to the Lord's Table* on the Internet at www.FinalCommand.org at significant discounts. Order one copy for each youth and older adult member. Because of the personal application questions throughout, I do not recommend that a couple or family try to share one copy. I've tried to keep your costs low so that every member can have his or her own copy without it becoming a financial burden. Order books several weeks or a month in advance of your scheduled start time to allow for any contingencies like books being out of stock. If you have a large congregation, contact the publisher about preparing a customized edition just for your church. Quantities of 3,000 or more might justify a special edition with a forward from you.

Invite the People. In the Old Testament sacred assemblies (especially the emergency ones that often led to revival), all the people were expected to attend. Because the Lord's Table was instituted for the Body of Christ, <u>make a special effort to get every member to participate in preparation and in attendance</u>. This study holds great potential as a time of renewal or revival among your members. I suggest that you send a personal letter to each member family and strongly encourage their participation and attendance. Encourage participation from the pulpit and through regular church information channels. You might even use a phone call campaign to assure every member knows the value and seriousness of this time of sacred assembly. Prepare a special sermon to extend the initial invitation to sacred assembly. "Blow the trumpet in Zion, declare a holy fast, call a sacred assembly" (Joel 2:15).

Distribute the Books. Distribute books to members **at least two weeks (three is better) prior to the date of the Lord's Table service**. You may want to start even earlier so people will have time to catch up if they should miss a lesson or two. When you distribute books, ask members to fill in the days and dates for your events on page 112.

Plan the Services. Coordinate plans for the services with other leaders (like music, drama, audiovisual). Make a special effort to make the worship experiences especially meaningful and memorable. Encourage planners to be creative in designing the atmosphere and experiences.

Consider Using <u>Final Command Action Manual</u> as a Follow-up Study. On page 108 is a description of the *Final Command* resource. The Lord's Table may set the stage for a fresh calling of your church to obedience to the Great Commission (Final Command) to make disciples of the nations. Set before your people the battle cry of the Moravians who experienced renewal at a Lord's Supper service: "To win for the Lamb that was slain, the reward of His sufferings" (p. 39). Let the love of Christ compel them (2 Cor. 5:14) to this ministry of reconciliation. Call them to a fresh surrender and obedience to the Lord's command.

Future Use of <u>Come to the Lord's Table</u>. After using this book your first time, you may want to encourage members to use it as a review for future celebrations of the Lord's Table. Your church may want to encourage an annual review of *Come to the Lord's Table* in years to come and encourage newcomers to complete the study in preparation for the time of sacred assembly at the Lord's Table.

Pre-Communion Service

A pre-Communion Service is a time for members to gather together and help each other make final preparations for the Lord's Table. It affords a time for members to pray together and for each other, reconcile relationships that may be broken, confess and seek forgiveness for publicly known sin, and in meaningful ways recommit their lives to the Lordship of Christ. Though you could celebrate the Lord's Table without having a pre-Communion service, I highly recommend that you give serious consideration to providing some time for members to prepare together.

The Bible does not give any set description of what must be done to fully prepare for the Lord's Table. Through this book, I've tried to guide your people to prepare personally. You could benefit as a church to have a time set aside before the Lord's Table to make some final preparations together. Below I've suggested some elements that might be part of a pre-Communion service. Ask the Lord to guide you in preparing for this service. Customize a service for your church—you have great latitude in what the service is like. Include the elements you sense would be most helpful for your church. If this is all new to you, you will find yourself walking by faith—and that is a good way to walk. Trust the Lord to guide you. If you sense a need for help, invite a fellow pastor or a denominational leader to assist you this first time.

Who should come? In the Old Testament sacred assemblies they invited all who could understand. Older children, youth, and adults would certainly be included. Even younger children can benefit by seeing adults taking their faith and relationships with Christ and His church seriously. Ask them to come for an open-ended period of time. You may want to hire some childcare workers for babies and preschoolers so every adult member can participate in the service.

Fasting Before Supper. I've suggested to members that they may want to fast before the Lord's Table. You may want to include this invitation to those who choose to fast to begin their fast by skipping the meal just prior to the pre-Communion service and continuing until the Lord's Table. This should not be legalistic, public, or mandatory. Allow personal freedom here.

Service Elements

Choose from the following elements to design your service or plan your own activities as God guides you.

- **Music and Singing:** sing hymns or provide special music related to the cross, atonement, the Lord's Supper, forgiveness, the love of Christ, and so forth.
- **Scripture Reading:** Read Scriptures related to the same topics. Include others that may call for members to deal seriously with specific sins. Consider responsive readings of Scriptures also.
- **Message:** If you preach, use a brief message on the importance of preparing to partake of the Lord's Table in a worthy manner and invite members to finalize their preparations for the Supper. Keep in mind that the focus of this service is on <u>response</u> to the Lord not just teaching and learning. Use the message to call for response and reserve most of your time for response.
- **Testimonies:** Invite individual testimonies about ways God has been working in lives during the preparations for the Lord's Table including experience of God's love and grace, a spiritual breakthrough, a victory over a besetting sin, reconciled relationships, confession of newfound faith in Christ, and so forth. As pastor, you may hear testimonies from members prior to the service. Enlist some of these persons to share their testimonies. Consider dividing into smaller groups of 4 to 8 and encourage members to share what God has done in their lives during this time of preparation.
- **Prayer:** Provide for a variety of prayer experiences.
  - Provide soft music for a time of silent prayer and meditation.
  - Someone could sing (or play a recorded version) "The Altar" by Ray Boltz and Steve Millikan and open your altar for individuals, couples, or families to come, kneel, and pray.
  - Break into smaller groups of 4 to 8 preferably members of the same sex. Invite members in each group to ask each other the question, "How may we pray for you?" Then have one or two in the group pray for each request. Requests might include:
    - ❑ besetting sin that I can't get victory over
    - ❑ broken relationship that must be mended (unforgiveness, bitterness, need to make restitution, etc.)
    - ❑ wounded spirit because of my past that keeps me at a distance from the heavenly Father
    - ❑ unbelief   ❑ wrong motives
    - ❑ prayerlessness   ❑ apathy

- ❑ disobedience ❑ moral failure
- ❑ pride ❑ too busy
- ❑ worldliness ❑ materialism, love for world

  – Provide opportunity for people to come and share a need or confess a sin and pray with a pastor, a minister, elder, deacon, or prayer warrior. If appropriate, share some of these needs with the congregation and invite some members to come and surround the person with prayer.

- **Public Confession:** The general guideline for public confession of sin is to confess the sin as broadly as the offense. Reserve public confession for sin that has become publicly known or sin that is against the church or many of the members. I recommend that the pastor personally screen each person's desire for public confession and make sure it is appropriate. Those receiving people for prayer should agree on a procedure to follow regarding public confession. Following a confession, guide the congregation to express their forgiveness, invite the person to pray aloud and ask God for forgiveness, invite some members to gather around him or her and pray for mercy and victory, or in some other way respond to the request for forgiveness.

- **Reconciling Relationships:** Encourage members to go to each other to ask forgiveness or to be reconciled over offenses God has identified this week. Provide soft music. Ask those who are not sensing a need to reconcile to pray for their fellow church members who are needing to forgive and be reconciled. Don't rush this time. You may want to share guidelines similar to these:

  – If you are the offender, acknowledge your sin and say, "Please forgive me." Don't give excuses or try to justify your actions. Don't imply or make accusations about wrong on the other person's part. That is their responsibility.

  – If you sense a broken relationship exists and don't know what is wrong, say, "I sense that there may be a broken relationship between us, but I'm not sure I know why. Help me understand what I need to do to be reconciled with you."

  – If you miss getting to reconcile with anyone, contact him or her after the service.

- **Invitation to Receive Christ:** Often in history, people were converted during the season of preparation for the Lord's Table. You may want to extend an invitation for anyone who chooses to confess their faith in Christ.

- **Open-ended Closing:** As you close the service, invite members to continue responding to the Lord as long as needed. They may want to remain for prayer, continue seeking to reconcile relationships, or to seek out prayer with one of the leaders.

LOVE FEAST (AGAPE MEAL)

The New Testament indicates that the churches had a meal time they called a love feast or *agape* (Greek word for *love*) meal. We don't have much indication of the details of what took place at these meals, but they were something more than an observance of the Lord's Supper. Some groups in history have experienced wonderful Christian fellowship and love at times they called a "love feast."

Again, this is an optional activity to add to your experience of the Lord's Table. Consider gathering for a love feast at the conclusion of the final week of lessons in *Come to the Lord's Table* (or soon thereafter). The following are ideas and suggestions you might consider in planning your meal.

- **Meal:** The meal can be simple or complex. Moravians serve a sweet bun and a cup of coffee for their love feasts. You could have a more extensive meal, a potluck meal, or a full blown "dinner on the grounds." One key to keep in mind is that the fellowship is to be the emphasis, not the food. Don't just eat and leave.
- **Singing:** The service should be light and more spontaneous than structured. Consider conducting a hymn sing and sing requests, favorites, or songs that focus on the love of Christ and our unity and Christian love for one another.
- **Testimonies:** Invite testimonies of what God has done in the past four-week focus on the Lord's Table. Start by asking members to share testimonies around their table or in a small group of about eight. These should be voluntary so don't just go around the circle. These could include victories won over sin, lives changed, relationships reconciled, deeper experiences of the love of Christ, experiences from a date or outing with the heavenly Father, experiences during the walk with Jesus (Week 3, Day 3), insights gained into the sacrifice of Christ, feelings and memories of the Lord's Table service itself, and so forth. After members have shared in small groups, call for some testimonies to be shared with the large group.
- **Affirmations:** Too often we fail to say thank you or to affirm what God is doing in and through those around us. Provide an opportunity for public "thank you's" or for affirmation of what members see

in the lives of others that is a blessing. Invite people to finish this sentence: "I thank God for ___(name)___ because…" You might even recognize some groups of people for a group "thank you." (like teachers, workers with preschoolers, ushers or others who may seldom get a thank you from the Body of Christ for their ministry to the Body). Think of other ways for members to express love and appreciation for the members of the Body of Christ.

- **Love Offering:** If you decide to give opportunity for a love offering, announce the opportunity early in the Lord's Table study or at least by the time of the Lord's Table so people will have time to reflect, pray, and prepare. Invite members to consider giving a special love offering above their regular giving to express an extra "thank you" to Christ for His sacrifice. Decide in advance how you will use this special offering. You might use it for benevolent needs of church members (like the church in Acts did with gifts like that of Barnabas, Acts 4:32-37). You might use it for a special mission project. You might give it to a church on the mission field or to a needy church in your own city. If you are willing to manage it, this could be more than just money. People might choose to give other things of value for use by others in the Body of Christ or things that could be sold (like jewelry, a used car, stocks, volunteer service for a particular project, etc.). You might even suggest that people who have identified an "idol of the heart" that they need to give away (not something that should rather be destroyed because of its wickedness) might bring that as their offering. This offering could include a boat, a collection, "toys," material things that have captured one's love, etc. Whatever you do, let this be a matter of joy not obligation. Encourage your people to have fun deciding what to give and joy in blessing others as they use the gifts to show God's love to one another.
- **Prayers:** Invite volunteers to stand and pray prayers of thanksgiving, praise, adoration and love to Christ for His love and for the blessings of the past few weeks.

DISCIPLESHIP RESOURCES

The following resources developed in part by Claude King have been especially designed for use with small groups. Each resource has a place in helping believers grow and mature in their faith. These may help you and your church more fully to obey the final command by "teaching [disciples] to observe all things that I have commanded you" (Matt. 28:20). Here's a brief description and purpose for each.

FINAL COMMAND RESOURCES™

For the most up-to-date and complete listing of small group discipleship resources by Claude King or to place an order visit the web site at:
www.FinalCommand.org

Come to the Lord's Table: A Sacred Assembly of the Church by Claude King. Final Command Resources, 2001. This book is a three-week study to help the members of a church prepare themselves to celebrate the Lord's Supper or Communion in a worthy manner. The first week helps members review the meaning of the cross and remember the Lord's death until He comes. Week 2 guides members to examine themselves as preparation to partake in a worthy manner. The lessons after the Lord's Table help Christians focus on the manner of life they should live in light of the sacrifice Jesus made for them. My prayer is that we will return to our first love for Christ.

Final Command Action Manual by Claude King. Final Command Resources, 2001. This book is designed to help all Christians in your church work together to obey the final command of the Lord by participating in the process of making disciples. Members will work together to undertake seven actions to lead others to faith in Christ. Leader's material and a variety of use plans are included in this book. This book is especially prepared for introduction in a half day workshop or retreat. It is a natural next step following a use of *Come to the Lord's Table.*

LIFEWAY DISCIPLESHIP RESOURCES

> The following resources are available from
> LifeWay Christian Stores 1-800-448-8032
> or online at www.LifeWayStores.com

Concentric Circles of Concern: Seven Stages for Making Disciples by W. Oscar Thompson, Jr., Carolyn Thompson Ritzmann, and Claude V. King. Broadman & Holman Publishers, 1999. This 208-page book is filled with moving relational evangelism testimonies and guides individuals and small groups to understand and apply "Seven Stages for Making Disciples." Chapters include personal and small-group learning activities. Though not required for use with *Final Command*, it provides a valuable resource for explanation and illustration for pastors and small group leaders.

Experiencing God: Knowing and Doing the Will of God (workbook) by Henry T. Blackaby and Claude V. King. LifeWay Press, 1990. This 224-page 12-unit workbook guides individuals into an intimate and personal relationship with God through which they come to know and do His will. Small groups will learn to function as the Body of Christ as they follow God's will together. Leaders will need a copy of the following leader's guide.

Experiencing God Leader's Guide by Claude V. King. LifeWay Press, 1990. This 64-page book provides resources and small group learning activities for a study of *Experiencing God* workbook. A wide variety of other *Experiencing God* resources are available from LifeWay Press.

Experiencing God (trade paperback book) by Henry T. Blackaby and Claude V. King, Broadman & Holman Publishers, 1994.

Fresh Encounter: God's Pattern for Revival and Spiritual Awakening by Henry T. Blackaby and Claude V. King. LifeWay Press, 1993. This 96-page workbook leads individuals in a six-week study of God's pattern in Scripture and history for revival and spiritual awakening. It provides a biblical call to repentance and return to the Lord. *Fresh Encounter* can help individuals and churches return to the Lord and reestablish the foundations necessary for fruitfulness in reaching a lost world. A church is encouraged to study this course all at the same time and in small groups as they seek to experience genuine revival as a church. Leaders will need a copy of the following leader's manual. Churches will benefit from the additional resources in the leader's kit.

Fresh Encounter Leader's Manual by Henry T. Blackaby and Claude V. King. LifeWay Press, 1993. This 120-page manual provides administrative suggestions for use of all the *Fresh Encounter* resources. It also provides small group learning activities for guiding the six-week study of the workbook described above.

Fresh Encounter Leader's Kit. LifeWay Press, 1993. This kit contains a copy of the workbook and leader's manual described above as well as an introductory video message to *Fresh Encounter* by Henry Blackaby, six 30-minute "plumb line" video messages by Henry Blackaby, a member's book for use with the plumb line messages, and twelve 30-minute audiocassette messages by Henry Blackaby and Avery Willis discussing leadership for times of revival and spiritual awakening.

Fresh Encounter (trade paperback book) by Henry T. Blackaby and Claude V. King, Broadman & Holman Publishers, 1996.

In God's Presence: Your Daily Guide to a Meaningful Prayer Life by T. W. Hunt and Claude V. King. LifeWay Press, 1994. This 96-page workbook is designed for a six-week study of prayer. Individuals learn six types of prayer by studying biblical examples and praying in their private devotions five days during the week. The built-in leader's guide helps a group learn to pray together in agreement. The small group meeting becomes a prayer meeting where members practice what they have been learning during the week. The goal of the study is to help churches become houses of prayer.

The Mind of Christ (workbook) by T. W. Hunt and Claude V. King. LifeWay Press, 1994. This 224-page workbook is a 12-week introduction to a lifelong process of becoming like Jesus Christ. Participants study the life and teachings of Christ and spend time in prayer and study as God works to renew their minds into the image of His Son. Small groups help members understand and apply truths to life so that the Body of Christ is pure and reveals Christlikeness to a lost world. Leaders will need a copy of the following leader's guide.

The Mind of Christ Leader's Guide by Claude V. King. LifeWay Press, 1994. This 64-page book provides resources and small group learning activities for a study of *The Mind of Christ* workbook.

The Mind of Christ Leader's Kit. LifeWay Press, 1994. The message of this course can be studied using the workbook above or through audiocassettes or videotapes where T. W. Hunt teaches the message in a conference setting. The kit includes the workbook, leader's guide, audiocassettes, a videotaped conference (6 hours), listening guide, and two one-hour worship videos on the Crucifixion and Resurrection of Christ. This kit is not required for the workbook study.

YOUR CHURCH'S SCHEDULE FOR THE LORD'S TABLE

EXPANDED FOUR-WEEK SCHEDULE

If your church plans on an expanded four-week study of *Come to the Lord's Table*, write below your church's scheduled days and dates for each of the following events.

❶ Start Studying Week 1: Day 1 of *Come to the Lord's Table*:

(day/date) _____

✪ (PC) Pre-Communion (day/date) _____

★ (LT) Lord's Table (day/date) _____

♥ (LF) Love Feast (day/date) _____

Use one of the following calendar to mark the dates for your church's celebration of the Lord's Table. Write the weekdays (Sun. Mon., etc.) across the top of the calendar. Write the numbers for the days of the month. Then write in the dates for the special events. Pre-Communion will come sometime toward the end of your third week of study. The Lord's Table will come at the beginning of Week 4, and the Love Feast will be scheduled sometime after Week 4.

WEEKDAYS:							
❶			**WEEK 1 LESSONS**				
Day 1	Day 2	Day 3	Day 4	Day 5	Day 6	Day 7	
			WEEK 2 LESSONS				
Day 1		Day 2		Day 3		Day 4	
							✪PC
	Day 5		Day 6		Day 7		
★LT			**WEEK 3 LESSONS**				
Day 1	Day 2	Day 3	Day 4	Day 5	Day 6	Day 7	
♥LF							

YOUR CHURCH'S SCHEDULE FOR THE LORD'S TABLE

Use one of the following calendars to mark the dates for your church's celebration of the Lord's Table. If your observance will take place on a Sunday, use calendar 1. If you plan for a Maundy Thursday observance during Easter Week use calendar 2. If you plan for an observance on a different day of the week prepare a similar calendar to schedule your study. On the calendar write the numbers for the days of the month. Then write in the dates for the special events.

Calendar 1: Sunday

SUN.	MON.	TUES.	WED.	THURS.	FRI.	SAT.
			WEEK 1			
Day 1	Day 2	Day 3	Day 4	Day 5	Day 6	Day 7
			WEEK 2			
Day 1	Day 2	Day 3	Day 4	Day 5	Day 6	Day 7
★LT			WEEK 3			
Day 1	Day 2	Day 3	Day 4	Day 5	Day 6	Day 7

✪ (PC) (Optional) Pre-Communion Day (date) _____
★ (LT) Lord's Table   (date) _____
♥ (LF) (Optional) Love Feast   (date) _____

CALENDAR 2: MAUNDY THURSDAY

SUN.	MON.	TUES.	WED.	THURS.	FRI.	SAT.
				WEEK 1		
				Day 1	Day 2	Day 3
				WEEK 2		
Day 4	Day 5	Day 6	Day 7	Day 1	Day 2	Day 3
				★LT	WEEK 3	
Day 4	Day 5	Day 6	Day 7	Day 1	Day 2	Day 3
Day 4	Day 5	Day 6	Day 7			